ANGELS TO ASHES
Largest Unsolved Mass Murder in Alaska History

MICHAEL MCGUIRE

authorHOUSE®

AuthorHouse™
1663 Liberty Drive
Bloomington, IN 47403
www.authorhouse.com
Phone: 1-800-839-8640

© 2010 Michael McGuire. All rights reserved.

No part of this book may be reproduced, stored in a retrieval system, or transmitted by any means without the written permission of the author.

First published by AuthorHouse 6/16/2010

ISBN: 978-1-4520-3825-4 (sc)
ISBN: 978-1-4520-3826-1 (hc)

Library of Congress Control Number: 2010908629

Printed in the United States of America
Bloomington, Indiana

This book is printed on acid-free paper.

Special Thanks
To

Marsha, whose inspiration allowed me to continue,

Anna, who patiently saw this to the end.

Tom and Anita, whose generosity I will never be able to re-pay.

The Coulthurst family.

Larry Demmert Jr.

And
All the families whose lives will never be the same.

Contents

Murder Aboard The Investor	1
Key Witness	3
Business As Usual	42
The Pipeline	45
The Trial I	48
Home Again	72
Trial II	103
My Investigation	114
Epilogue?	143

Murder Aboard The Investor

The fishing boat just seemed to appear from nowhere, having been shrouded in the dense fog that surrounded Craig Alaska in the early morning of September 5, 1982.

The 58 foot INVESTOR from Blaine Washington had been anchored in the same spot for over thirty hours, all the while hidden from view because of a September storm.

Nearly a mile to the south lays the fishing village of Craig, busy during this time of year as the salmon fishing season is winding down and other fisheries are gearing up. Fishermen are busy unloading the last of the seasons catch, cleaning the gear, getting paid, and of course getting out. Some stay for the last opening, but most are just glad they survived another season and are anxious to see families, sweethearts, or just relax.

It was not to be for the crew of the INVESTOR. The people in Craig said they noticed the INVESTOR sitting off in the distance, many say it was odd that the boat wasn't headed for the last opening due to begin the next day. All said that the INVESTOR was the first to arrive and the last to leave, "a hard working boat" was the term most used.

However, someone in Craig knew the INVESTOR and her entire crew would NEVER fish again. The INVESTOR had been left in the cove some thirty hours earlier, believing she would sink. Standing on the dock as the fog lifted the killer or killers would learn how the effort to scuttle the INVESTOR had failed. There she sat holding her ghostly cargo, a cargo once alive.

But they would try again.

By the time September 7th was over, this unknown or unknowns had taken so many chances, came so close to being caught, must have felt so desperate, so frightened, that he or they had no choice but to return to the INVESTOR. The floating coffin that had been left to vanish, was now pointing directly to someone on shore.

KEY WITNESS

The primary reason I became interested in this case was Larry Demmert Jr. I met Larry in the fall of 1985. I met him in Seaside Oregon. We immediately hit it off. Larry is a tall muscular young man with longish sandy hair. His native features and visible shyness just added to his boyish charm. Larry and I had several long conversations about all sorts of things. We talked about his fishing in Alaska, his family, his dreams. He talked a lot about his father, who had taught him all he knows about the Alaska waters.

He was very proud of the fact that he was the youngest person ever to receive a master's license. He had also been the youngest skipper of a commercial fishing boat in the State of Alaska.

Larry had talked of his trouble with drugs, especially valium. He told me of the gruesome murders aboard a fishing boat named the Investor which occurred in Craig Alaska. He told me that the Alaska State Troopers were considering him the KEY WITNESS, and he was going to testify at the trial which was to begin sometime in the near future. Larry went on to tell me that his valium usage had begun after he had become involved with the investigators who had been pressuring him regarding what and who he seen the night of the murders. Larry was very concerned as to the involvement of his lifelong friend. At the time he didn't mention any names and I didn't ask, however I could see that Larry was very concerned about what was going to happen in Ketchikan Alaska where the trial was scheduled to take place.

Larry told me that the detectives that were questioning him, they had in fact taken him to a motel for a period of about two weeks, during which time they had supplied him with valium and questioned him as to what he saw, who he saw, and repeated this over and over. He appeared very frightened and confused. He was torn between testifying against a boyhood friend, who he really believed he had in fact seen on the dock in Craig Alaska, holding a rifle the night of the gruesome slaughter of eight people aboard the Investor. This included two small children and the wife of the captain who was also pregnant at the time. Larry was torn between staying silent and living with the secret.

Growing up Larry had lived his life with the motto of "don't talk to cops, and don't be a snitch." The magnitude of this crime, and the pressure he was feeling from his conscience had Larry scared to death; he would be dammed if he did, and dammed if he didn't. Larry had been raised knowing right from wrong; his strong native heritage had instilled in him great work ethics as well as honesty. During this time Larry had become very apprehensive, he as well as his family had received some very threatening phone calls.

I had long talks with Larry; he stated on more than one occasion that all he wanted was "his life back." His whole routine had been shattered, his fishing season had been ruined, his family had been threatened, and his income had all but dried up. All he wanted was an assemblence of order; he knew that he would be put thru some real bad times at the trial. Larry said he was real scared. I told him that I would be there to support him if he wanted me to. He said he would let me know when he found out for sure when the trial was to begin.

He left for Alaska and I didn't hear from him for sometime.

It was sometime in February of 1986, when my phone rang. It was Larry, we chatted about what was going on, how his life was going, his sobriety, his family and just small talk. He then asked me if I was still willing to support him at the trial, of course I said yes, he then told me it was scheduled to begin in late February or early March. I told him that I would clear my schedule and be there when he needed me. I could feel the tension in his voice, it cracked as he said thank you.

I had no idea what then what I was about to be involved in.

Larry met me at the small airport in Ketchikan, Alaska. Getting there had already been an adventure. I had taken my own plane from Seaside Oregon to Seattle, then boarded an Alaska Airline flight to Anchorage, changed planes and arrived in Ketchikan sometime in the early evening. The airport in Ketchikan is on a small spit of land, almost an island; it was raining so hard that the visibility was almost zero. A heavy blanket of clouds lay over the ground looking like a scene from horror movie. Being a pilot myself, I was very impressed with the skill of the Alaska pilots.

I was told later that February can be the harshest month weather wise in Ketchikan. The rainfall average is about a half an inch to an inch a day. Larry warned me that when the rain lets up the wind and cold temperatures will get your attention. He went on to say that Ketchikan is still a pretty little town; he had been coming there since he was a small boy on his dads fishing boat.

Ketchikan is located on the shores of Revillagigedo Island, pressed right up against the mountains that seem to rise up from the sea. Most of the homes in Ketchikan are perched on hillsides; they just seem to appear from behind the beautiful green forest.

Larry had reserved me a room in the same motel that he was staying. After checking in, we went to the dining room for dinner. Larry appeared to be very nervous; we made small talk, talked about the flight in, the weather, just stuff. I stopped the conversation; I asked Larry what was really going on. With a long pause, Larry started to cry, trying to hold back his tears it was obvious that he was in distress. I just waited; finally Larry looked up and started to talk. He said he missed his family, was worried about missing the fishing season, all of his so called friends had walked away from him and he said he felt threatened.

It was about 8:30, the rain had stopped, so we decided to take a walk downtown. The town occupies the only level land in Ketchikan. As we walked Larry pointed out some of the sights, the boardwalk that used to be the only way to walk around town due to the ankle deep mud that followed the heavy rains. The boardwalk had since been replaced with sidewalks; these were raised some two feet from road level, again because of the sloppy weather. Larry spoke to some people as we walked, nodded to others, nobody really stopped to sincerely ask him how he was, and nobody really showed much concern. I could see that this was hurting Larry, after all he used to play on these streets with the local kids, now he was here, alone and scared.

Right on schedule the rain began to pour. Larry and I caught a cab back to the motel. Once there I made my way to my room to unpack, the rooms were comfortable yet sparse. Toward the window was a small round table with two wooden chairs, opposite the table was a cabinet which held an old TV. The desk was a one piece desk and luggage holder. Looking around the room, it would serve the purpose. After all I was only going to be here a couple of days, then back home to Seaside and my normal life.

The phone rang and it was Larry, suggesting that we have some coffee in his room. He said his room was only two doors down from mine. I said I would be down in a few minutes. Arriving at Larry's room it appeared to be already much lived in, he had been here two days and the room had an appearance of boredom and confusion. On the round table sat a large three ring binder, it took up the whole table, and I asked Larry what it was? He said"look at it" as I opened it I saw it was testimony from Larry, testimony from his Grand Jury appearance, it seemed it was almost written as a script. "That's the shit they want me to remember" that's what they want me to say tomorrow, Larry said. It's a lot of testimony, I replied, yea and most of it's not true, most of it is twisted, almost like they tried to put words in my mouth, Larry replied, they really want to hang John. John? I said, yes, John Peel, Larry said, I don't think they even looked at anybody else for this crime. Those fucking Troopers fucked this up from the get go, Larry said, as he sat down on the edge of the bed.

How so, I asked. Oh, shit Mike they wanted to pin this on me in the beginning. They questioned everybody, they snuck around they wasted so much time. I told them what I had seen the night of the murders; they just blew me off in the beginning, when they couldn't find anyone who could really identify the killer they just started putting together this bullshit story.

Do you think this Peel guy is the killer? I asked. Larry said without hesitation, "Yea" he did it; I know he did it, but he wasn't alone, he isn't smart enough to have done this alone, he hasn't got the balls." The troopers say that drugs weren't involved, that's bullshit too.

There were a lot of drugs in Craig, The Investor was a known drug boat in the past, yet for some reason the District Attorney has decided that the drug rumors aren't worthy of investigation. I think she is getting advice from someone who doesn't want the truth to be known. Hell there is even rumors she is having an affair with on of the troopers. Mike, this is a real cluster fuck and I'm right in the middle.

It was getting late, and I was tired, so I told Larry I'd meet him for breakfast and go to the courthouse with him in the morning. I returned to my room, and because of the time difference I needed to call home. Tomorrow is my wife's birthday and I won't be there, so I need to call and wish her well.

The Investigation
Craig, Alaska
Tuesday, September 7, 1982

The fishing boat just seemed to appear. Showing larger as the sun burned away the dense fog that had hidden the 58-foot fishing boat named the Investor. The boat was out of Blaine Washington, she had been anchored in the same spot for over 30 hours, hidden from view by the fog and foul weather.

Just north of the border of British Columbia, Canada, off the coast of Alaska and just opposite the town of Ketchikan, is Prince of Wales Island, part of the Alexander Archipelago that forms the "Inside Passage" this string of islands acts as a buffer against the northern Pacific Ocean. On the west side of Prince of Wales Island, off Iphigenia Bay is the small fishing port of Craig.

The people of Craig noticed the Investor sitting off in the distance. The people thought it strange that the boat wasn't heading for the last salmon opening of the season due the next day.

One man maybe more knew that the Investor and her crew would not be going to fish the opener; in fact they knew that the Investor and her crew would never fish again.

They had left the boat some 30 hours earlier, believing she would sink. As the fog lifted they would learn how the effort to scuttle the Investor had failed.

For there she sat holding her ghostly cargo, a cargo that was once alive.

But they would try again. By the time September, 7th 1982 was over these unknown men who had taken so many chances, came so close to being caught, must have felt so desperate that they had no choice but to send someone back to the Investor, back to the floating coffin that was now pointing at them as they stood somewhere on the shore.

The explosions were heard in the town center, flames shot 30 feet into the air, the smoke could be seen for miles.

The fishing vessel Investor was now ablaze in a cove between Fish Egg Island and Cole Island off Craig, about 50 miles from Ketchikan.

People in Craig said the investor **pulled into the docks on September 5 and tied up in the North Cove harbor. What happened after that, from Sunday evening to Tuesday afternoon**, was pieced together by two Alaska state troopers.

The investor was owned by Mark Coulthurst, she was a new 58 foot seiner, valued somewhere between $750,000 and $1 million. She was the pride and joy of the Coulthurst family. Coulthursts partner was his wife, Irene. They had met in high school and have been married since 1974, at the time of the murders. They had two small children, daughter Kimberly age 5 and son John age 4, Irene was also thought to be pregnant at the time. On board, the investor on this day was the crew; Dean Moon of Blaine Washington had been on the investor crew for three years. He was 19 years old. Moon was described by friends as hard working. Dean Moon was in charge of running the Investors skiff. This was the 20 ft boat powered by a large diesel engine it is used to assist pulling the nets once the set was completed. People said that Dean admired Coulthurst and wanted to follow his lead.

The second crewman was Mike Stewert, 19 of Bellingham Washington, he was Coulthurst cousin and had only been onboard the Investor since June, he was attending college in Washington and studying pre-law.

Another crewman was Chris Heyman, 18 of San Rafael California, he had been hired on the Investor because of a friendship that his father had with Coulthurst. The last crewman was Jerome Keown a friend of Dean Moon he had only been aboard the Investor since August 26th; he also was to begin college in the fall.

These were the eight people, five men, a woman, and two young children. This is the ghostly cargo that lay aboard the Investor.

Smoke was coming from the hull thick and black at first then the fire caught hold and the flames engulfed the entire vessel. When the first call for help came folks onshore started scrambling, trying to find anything that would take them to the scene , boats that were already out started to converge on the spot about a quarter mile south of Cole Island.

By the time the first boats had arrived at the scene, it appeared that the section of the Investor that housed the living area was completely engulfed in flames. Flames could be seen in her wheelhouse. By now the Investor was fully engulfed in a raging inferno.

" There is no way we can get close enough to do anything to help" the skipper of the fishing vessel Casino remembers, the Casino was the first boat on the scene, "the fire was so intense I wasn't able to get within fifty feet" said the skipper. "Boarding the boat would have been impossible. Just then a small skiff arrived and was circling the Investor "look for anyone alive" the skipper of the Casino remembers yelling to the skiff. The skiff circled several times but was unable to see anything, nothing was moving aboard the Investor.

The fire continued to spread the entire length of the boat, from the enclosed cabin and wheel house it was now to the outside, the seine nets were now smoldering and about to erupt. Within fifteen minutes the entire back deck was engulfed with flames that were 15 feet high. With no possible way to fight the inferno the boats and the people that had rushed to the scene, now just bobbed helplessly watching in horror, thinking the worst.

Alaska State Trooper Bob Anderson was the first of many law enforcement agents to arrive on the scene. He had received a call that was relayed from the Coast Guard at 4:20 that evening telling him that a boat was on fire outside Craig, about seven miles from his office in the small town of Klawock. That was all the information Anderson received. As Anderson was arriving in Craig he could see a large vessel, just off the tip of Fish Egg Island, from what he could see the boat was totally ablaze. Anderson's first thought was that the boat had been set on fire by it's disgruntled owner, the season was over, maybe he had a bad catch, maybe it was for the insurance money.

When Anderson arrived in Craig his first action was to find anything that might help fight the fire, something, anything. The Craig fire department was new and didn't have any firefighting equipment that was able to fight a fire on the water. Not wasting any time, Anderson tried to use the 26 foot boat that belonged to Alaska Fish & Wildlife; he again found this useless both batteries were dead. Anderson's last effort was his personal boat that was moored nearby. Arriving at the scene Anderson came upon several boats in all shapes and sizes. The weather was overcast, seas were calm. Looking at the scene, Anderson quickly learned that attempts to put the fire out were being done by one lone fisherman a heroic effort; the man had been able to get close enough to the inferno to unhook the anchor of the Investor and try to tow her closer to shore.

By now the fire was consuming the entire boat, the heat was intense, the walls of the cabin and wheelhouse were falling in, and the fiberglass was like molten lava, the mast caved in under its own weight slowly almost as if it was saluting its dead cargo. The situation was totally out of control. Anderson now was nothing but a spectator.

The Tug Andy Head rushed to the scene and arrived around six in the evening almost two hours had passed since the first May Day call had been received. The tug had only one pump, she managed to get close enough to put water on the nets, with that done the water was directed to the main cabin, this endeavor proved to be much more difficult. The Coast Guard was contacted and a request for additional pumps to be airlifted to the scene was given. The Investor now started to list to her starboard side, it look like a bull moose rolling over after being shot.

Anderson, seeing that he was helpless at the scene returned to Craig to call his superior. Sergeant John Glass was in Ketchikan at the time, Anderson said "the fire was no accident" he told Glass that according to witnesses the "fire just spread to fast", "it was arson, I'm sure of it." Sergeant Glass prepared to send an arson investigator to the scene.

Once back on shore Trooper Anderson tried to learn as much about the burning boat as he could. He learned that the boat was called the

Investor out of Blaine Washington, the owner was Mark Coulthurst. The Investor had been fishing out of Petersburg, Alaska. People in Craig that knew the Coulthursts thought that the wife Irene Coulthurst and the two children had returned home so the children could start school. Anderson directed the Coast Guard as well the Craig police to find the whereabouts of the family.

Anderson was also informed by the Craig police that the skiff belonging to the Investor had been located at the cold storage dock. The skiff had been seen coming from the direction of the Investor fire. Upon examination of the skiff, a nozzle from what appeared to be a gas can had been discovered in the bottom of the skiff. Once more pointing to arson. At seven thirty the Coast Guard got a call from the tug Andy Head saying that the fire was contained, brought under control. The Coast Guard also reported that something suspicious had been found, something that may have been used to set the fire. Trooper Anderson agreed to return to the scene as soon as he was able to do so.

Once back at Ben's Cove, Anderson found the Investor completely burned to the gunnels; the fiberglass portion was melted layer upon layer much like a laminated piece of plywood. What the Coast Guard had found was a pail, a pail that may have been used to carry an accelerant, upon further inspection Anderson came to the conclusion that the pail had come from the wheelhouse, and it had been used to hold sponges and cleaning supplies.

Anderson concluded that the fire was contained and the water had cooled the hull enough for a preliminary investigation. Slipping on heavy gloves and a pair of boots he had borrowed from someone on the tug Andy Head. Anderson and some volunteers stepped aboard the charred wreckage. The black areas which were a mixture of charcoal and melted fiberglass were as slick as ice; the boat had listed 20 degrees or more toward starboard, making it almost impossible to make any headway.

Anderson's intention was to do a preliminary investigation before he ran out of daylight; it was now almost eight o' clock, a full four hours since the fire was discovered. The full investigation would have to wait for the arson experts. One of the volunteers had gone into the area where the galley had been; as he proceeded he noticed something oozing up between the layers of scorched fiberglass. The volunteer said it looked "like a gel of some sort", almost like pie filling. Anderson knelt down to take a closer look, his eyes noticed something big, and he thought it may be a carcass of a deer with the feet sticking straight out. There was just some burnt tissue and some gut hanging out, whatever it was it was totally not discernable. Stepping back Anderson realized he was looking at human remains. Upon lifting another layer of burnt fiberglass another body was discovered. Trooper Anderson now found himself standing in the middle of a crime scene, a scene that was so gruesome, so unthinkable; it was about to get much worse.

Trooper Anderson couldn't remove either of the bodies without permission of the coroner. The only coroner that would respond was in Ketchikan, not wanting to sound an alarm over the radio Anderson was careful in his message. "Found two, could be more," "Permission to remove." It didn't take long before a response came from the coroner, "proceed."

Anderson returned to the place where he had found body number two. As he lifted that body he found another, directly beneath it, the two victims had been pressed against each other. The one on top was a large male, recognizable because he was not burned as badly as the first body they had discovered; he appeared to have short hair. At first glance he appeared to have gunshot wound to the head. The body on the bottom was also an adult, the figure looked like a women.

As Anderson continued his direction was port side, where the cabin walls had melted and collapsed, he came across the remains which appeared to be a small child or a baby, totally unrecognizable, the body count was now at four.

Removing the smaller body was difficult; pieces of tissue fell off when it was moved. As the bodies were removed they were taken to the cannery dock at Columbia Ward Fisheries in Craig. Upon arriving at the dock Anderson noticed that a small crowd had begun to gather.

The removal of the bodies was tedious, the tide was at its lowest for the day and the bodies had to be placed on pallet boards, and then lifted by crane. From there they were lowered to a waiting cart and wheeled into the warehouse where they were locked up for the night.

Anderson was about to return home for the night, knowing full well that sleep was out of the question, after all how could he sleep after what had encountered. A Craig policeman approached Anderson and said that someone had seen an individual coming from the scene in a power skiff; he had been spotted just after the fire had been reported. Anderson inquired if it would be possible to talk to the fellow in the morning?

"He's going back to the Lower 48 in the morning, he's returning to college", the officer replied. "He's leaving on the first flight out in the morning". Asked to describe the man, the witness said he had light brown or maybe blonde hair and was wearing a baseball cap that had a logo on it. Anderson asked if the witness could tell the age of the skiff operator. The witness said maybe between 20 and 21 about the same age as "I am" he estimated his weight to be about 150-160 lbs stocky and he was wearing glasses, he couldn't tell how tall he was because he was sitting down. "I still got a pretty good look at him; our boats were only a few yards apart.

After the interview Anderson returned to the dock to look at the skiff, briefly examining it, he came to the conclusion that the rain had washed away any evidence, fingerprints would be impossible.

He decided to leave it where it was. Anderson didn't realize it was the skiff from the Investor. He felt it was only important because it had been seen coming from the direction of the fire.

↘

In Craig Alaska there are three bars, where anything and everything takes place, almost like Alice's restaurant. The rumors had already begun spreading; the sense of fear could be felt in all three. The three bars held its own particular customers, loyal to the core, fishermen and loggers and Alaska road crews gathered at the Hill Bar; known to locals as "The Hill." a little strange a little dingy, a wall of windows that had a view of the public float and just two blocks from downtown. The Hill also was the roughest bar in Craig. On weekends it was nothing to have a large brawl breakout, usually loggers, against road crews, against fishermen.

The local natives many of them the Tlingits and Haidas from Prince of Wales Island claimed the Craig Inn. The Craig Inn is more subdued, far less rowdy but rougher around the edges. The Craig Inn has very few windows, natural light was nonexistent, and the bar was long and behind it stood a wall of dusty booze bottles. The floor was well worn wood; years of loggers with cork boots had left their mark. A clientele of ex-cons, drug dealers, and other not so clean individuals mingled with the locals.

The third watering hole was called Ruth Ann's; it was referred to as "up town", dark and warm, brass railings all but the ferns. The food was above average and the menu was more than three items long.

Rumors and speculation were running wild, the number of dead changed with every conversation. But four were confirmed dead and the reality was just that, people had died this day in the small village of Craig. The smell of fear was in the air, and paranoia had everybody on edge. Each rumor topped the next; they flew like seagulls around the fish dock.

Rumors of the Coulthursts having a knock down drag out fight, rumors of angry crewmembers, rumors of money owed to investors. Then there were rumors of missing drugs, lots of drugs, and later rumors about organized crime. All these rumors were just that, people in Craig really didn't know the victims; the Investor rarely came into Craig and didn't sell to the local canneries. The Investor usually sold its fish in the Petersburg area. The Investor had little reason to be there this time, it was only there because it was near the end of the season, and the last opening was just a few days away.

The waitresses at Ruth Ann's were in shock, they remembered the Coulthursts well. Two days before this tragedy Mark Coulthurst had come in with his three and a half month pregnant wife and two kids to celebrate his twenty-eighth birthday. "They seemed happy" one of the staff told investigators later, but were they? The cook insisted that Mark Coulthurst had argued with a patron, the cook thought it might have been over money. One of the waitresses remembers a patron who was rude and loud; he had arrived late and got in her way several times as she tried to clear tables in the small crowded restaurant. The staff realized they may have been the last people to see the Coulthurst's alive. At the city float, Brice Anderson and Jan Kittleson were taking extreme precautions to protect themselves. Earlier that evening they had gone to the Craig police department to report what they had seen as they rushed toward the Investor fire. They were trying to be responsible people; they thought they had seen something that might be important. They told the police they had seen "a guy speeding away from the burning boat in a skiff". They had gone out of their way to try to stop the skiff; they wanted to know if anyone was on the boat. They tried to tell the skiff operator that the boat was owned by a friend of theirs. They told the police they almost had to ram the skiff to make it slow down. The operator of the skiff said" Yeah, there's people on the boat. "Then he just sped away" the pair said. They told police that they were tied up at the city float. We are aboard the Casino. The police assured the couple that someone would contact them, because the people on board the Investor had been murdered. The news came as a shock, the couple had barely considered the possibility that their friends were aboard the boat, they had even talked to each other about how they had been hopeful that no one was found in the water.

Now staring them in the face, was the fact that they knew something they wish they didn't. They may have seen the killer, the mass murderer, they had seen him. They had been within feet; they had even talked to him. All night Jan and Bruce tried to recall small details about who and what they had encountered. They soon realized that they didn't recall the same things. Bruce wasn't sure what the skiff operator looked like, Jan recalled that the man wore glasses and thought the man was very young, maybe in his twenties. The night was spent trying to piece together what they had really seen, trying desperately to recall the smallest detail.

Orders were given to ship the bodies out on the first plane to Ketchikan, that flight was scheduled to leave at 10am. Incoming on that flight were two State Troopers, Captain Mike Kolivosky, the commander of the "A" detachment of the Alaska State Troopers, headquartered in Juneau, and Lieutenant Roger McCoy his deputy commander. Kolivosky was a boisterous, cigar chewing no non-sense kind of guy. McCoy was more methodical paid more attention to detail. As they approached from the air they were able to spot the Investor, and were able to see the boat was still on fire.

The two new arrivals were met by Trooper Anderson and Jerry Mackie a former Public Safety Officer who was responsible for search and rescue and law enforcement when Anderson was out of town. Upon arrival at the dock they boarded Mackie's boat and headed straight to the scene of the crime. As they approached Ben's Cove they came upon the gruesome sight, The Investor was listing on her starboard side, they noticed that is was a very dangerous situation, the Investor could "roll anytime" Kolivosky muttered.

Worried that crucial evidence could compromised by the continuous fire Kolivosky wanted the fire put out immediately. The Craig fire chief who was at the scene suggested firefighting foam and was quickly shut down. He was told the fire was outside his jurisdiction. Trooper Anderson had remembered a logging crew had a helicopter that was used for fighting forest fires. The helicopter was summoned and began dumping sea water on the hull of the Investor. The helicopter had a five hundred gallon water bucket which sent its load crashing down upon the hull of the Investor, the boat shook under the strain of this massive pounding. The fire was not going to go out easily; the helicopter made at least five passes before the fire finally gave way. Seeing that the fire was extinguished the Troopers returned to Craig, nothing more could take place at the scene until the arson investigator arrived. What strikes me strange is that the Investor was left unguarded, open to anyone. Evidence was left to the sea air, and the tides. With every wave that rolled over the Investor valuable evidence was being compromised.

In the town of Craig the troopers had another problem; they had to find witnesses to this crime. The first place they started was the city float. The crew aboard the fishing boat Casino was of particular interest. The couple's description of the skiff operator that they saw returning from the scene was of great interest to Lieutenant McCoy. The Casino captain Bruce Anderson supplied more answers that did his crewmate. Again they described a young man in his early to mid twenties, light brown or blonde hair and wearing old black rimmed glasses and a baseball cap. They did provide some additional information. According to Anderson, Mark Coulthurst had said that the Investor had "a crew of five people plus his wife and family." The captain of the Casino also said that Coulthurst stated that the Investor "was immaculate and unbelievably equipped". Fire suppressant systems were state of the art. Anderson said the fire had taken off to quickly, maybe some sort of "accelerant had been used" he told McCoy.

The witnesses said the skiff operator operated the skiff with skill, "he knew what he was doing" Anderson said, he seemed to know the area also, he maneuvered around the maker buoy so as not to run aground.

Both witnesses stated that the skiff man wasn't a familiar crewman, they knew that for sure.

The troopers knew that there was only three ways off the Island: by plane, by boat or by a ferry that left from the other side of Prince of Wales. Checking with the airline was the first thing they did, inquiring if anyone matching the description they had of the skiff operator had taken a flight out of Craig. They checked with the ferry terminal in Hollis which was thirty miles on the other side of the island. The local police were given a description of the suspect.

Of the officers involved, Jerry Mackie was the most familiar with Craig and the people who lived there. Like most everyone he was stunned that a crime of this sort had happened in his town. Everyone including himself was on edge. It wasn't known exactly how many people had died aboard the Investor, one thing was clear, they had been murdered.

Trooper Mackie had work to do, he checked the Tyee Airlines terminal, the manager there was positive that no one matching the description had taken a flight out that morning or even the day before. Mackie then proceeded to the Hill Bar, not sure of what kind of reception he would receive even though his mother owned the bar. He tried not to call any undue attention to himself, and he just looked around, trying to make eye contact with each person. Most of the patrons didn't even look up from their beers, however one man caught Mackie's attention, "just something about him, and he seemed nervous, shifty, and even kinky". Mackie wasn't sure what set this guy apart, but he later stated this guy had "that look in his eye". Mackie couldn't describe what he felt just "chilling" he recounted. This is the guy, he told himself, he fits everything, size, color of his hair, age, he wasn't wearing glasses Mackie noted. Mackie summoned Troopers Kolivosky and McCoy, upon arriving at the Hill Bar, Kolivosky decided he would go in and see if he could notice the man in question, asking Mackie to point out the man thru the large window, Mackie noticed the man had moved from the center of the bar closer to the windows, this provided a better view of the streets and downtown Craig. Mackie pointed to the twenty something looking man sitting by himself at the bar, the one with dirty blonde hair.

The man kept looking at the troopers, just like he had when Mackie had cruised the bar the first time. Kolivosky entered the bar and walked up to the man, asking him to step outside, Kolivosky had the same uneasy feeling. "I need to see some identification" Kolivosky asked. The man reached into his right back pocket and produced his Washington State driver's license, the name on the license was John Kenneth Peel, Kolivosky explained why he was being questioned, someone had been seen leaving the Investor fire, and he fit the description. Mr. Peel said he knew the crew of the Investor, they were friends, he mentioned that he had worked for Mark Coulthurst in the past.

This man fit the description, what also bothered Kolivosky was that Mackie had picked him out of a crowded bar. Of all the people Mackie could have picked, this one was familiar with all on board the Investor. Captain Kolivosky entered his report for September 8th "1:20 pm. Attempt to locate witnesses. Hill Bar. John Peel. Possible suspect. Negative." Kolivosky's report aside, John Peel remained a "person of interest". In fact he was the only person from the start that garnered any attention.

Precious time was being wasted, Trooper Anderson remembered that another witness had said he had seen the skiff operator; maybe he could identify John Peel. They found the man near the cannery; they asked him to join them and took a walk down to the float dock. As they approached the dock they saw John Peel, he was standing on the float talking to the crew of the Libby 8, an old but sea worthy seiner. As the Troopers approached the float they stopped, Kolivosky pressed the man to take a good look at the people standing on the float, and do any of them look like the man you saw in the skiff? "No" the man said firm in his belief. Captain Kolivosky then pointed to John Peel, how about that guy? Kolivosky asked. Can you identify him as the man you saw operating the skiff?". "That's John Peel, I know him." The Troopers thanked the man for his time and let him go.

With nothing more concrete to go on, the Troopers split up. Anderson and the Chief of Police headed to the cannery dock, they wanted to know what John Peel was doing talking to the crew of the Libby 8. Upon arriving at the dock they noticed that only one man was visible, it seemed that the boat was being cleaned and readied for winter. The skipper of the Libby 8 was named Larry Demmert Jr. an Alaska Native who was known to the Chief of Police. After some pleasantries they asked Demmert if he knew John Peel?, Demmert said that Peel had crewed on the Libby 8, Demmert said little else. Trooper Anderson wanted to know where Peel was, Demmert said "I haven't seen John in a couple of days," Demmerts manner was cold and he didn't volunteer any information. The Police Chief had known Larry Demmert since they were kids. Never really got along with him or his family the Chief said later. Trooper Anderson sensed that Demmert was not forthcoming with all he knew about John Peel. The Chief later told Trooper Anderson "Mr. Demmert knows more than he's saying, I know Larry Demmert."

As the two investigators were leaving the dock they ran into another crew member of the Libby 8 Dawn Holstrom. Holstrom told them she knew some of the people aboard the Investor. She was visibly upset almost in shock. She was not able to speak without breaking down, there was nothing they could do, and she was unable to continue. The two men then headed to the Hill Bar. John Peel had disappeared.

Craig is so small, they figured they could talk to almost everyone in town in a few days, around every corner they saw someone who may be a witness, rumors were taking over the town, the murders were on everybody's lips. People were edgy and trust was fleeting, and time was running out. Anderson felt the investigation was becoming sidetracked; "sloppy" was the term he used.

Around four o'clock a float plane arrived from Ketchikan arrived, carrying with it two more investigators. The Criminal Investigation Bureau in Anchorage had sent Sergeant Chuck Miller who was a lead homicide investigator with the CIB. The second was Sergeant Jim Stogsdill, whose specialty was arson investigation. The were accompanied by Ketchikan prosecuting attorney Mary Ann Henry, her duties were to assist the troopers with search warrants, legal boundaries and whatever the troopers needed in the legal department. The town viewed these arrivals as a confirmation of the seriousness of the crime.

Miller was reported to be somewhat skeptical of the first reports, he even stated "probably those flakes in southeast Alaska, overreacting to a simple boat fire." Sergeant Glass of Ketchikan assured him it was anything but a routine fire. Although Sergeant Glass didn't know a great deal he did know that Mark Coulthurst his wife Irene and their two small children had been on board the Investor. Glass also had the names of the other crew members, Dean Moon, 19; Michael Stewart, 19: Chris Heyman, 18: and Jerome Keown, 19.

Sergeant Glass also was aware that four bodies they had recovered had been x-rayed in Ketchikan. The x-rays revealed metal fragments in some remains, possibly bullets.

The newly arrived investigators wanted to proceed to the scene as soon as possible. Arriving at the scene the troopers found the Investor still smoldering. Buckets of water soon did away with the flames and Miller and Stogsdill briefly surveyed the boat. They came to a conclusion that if the Investor was moved it would surely sink, they would loose any evidence that may still be available. The investigation would have to be done "where she lies" said Stogsdill.

Miller and Stogsdill made a list of what they would need to proceed. A float dock arrangement that could be tied up alongside the Investor, this would stabilize the boat as well as provide an area for the evidence to be sorted. Also on the list were shovels and screens that would be used for sifting charred debris, they also requested different sized evidence bags, knowing that this order might present a problem, they called upon the cannery for large plastic totes that were used to store fish would have to do.

Craig Alaska
September 9th to September 11th

Sergeant Miller and arson Investigator Stogsdill spent almost three days on the burn out Investor. The rain in September in southeast Alaska is almost daily, it falls like sheets blowing on a clothes line, almost sideways with a wind that seems to agitate it so it soaks everything that stands in the way. Clouds hang low and seem to spread a blanket just above the treetops. The sky is a gray, so gray it seems like the sunlight will never get through again. The rain numbs a person to his soul; you think you will never be warm again. These are the conditions that the investigators faced aboard the Investor.

Putting shovel loads of debris thru wire mesh they attempted to sort anything that looked like bone fragments or maybe teeth, anything that could possibly help identify who was on board. Burnt tissue recovered in chunks was also put through the screens and sifted. Stogsdill crawled on his hands and knees, trying no to overlook anything. On the portside of the hull they discovered more bones; it appeared to be ribs and maybe vertebrae.

On the second day, two men form Delta Marine arrived, they represented the boat builder. They examined the engine room where they found the aftermath of the fire damage. The room was filled with sorted oils and soot, the batteries had exploded, the fire system had gone off and left its own contribution of damage. As the boat builders continued to examine the engine room they made a surprising find. They noticed that all of the valves for the boats pumps had been opened, normally this was done to provide water for the refrigeration of the fish hold, where the fish were held. These valves would never be open allowing water into an empty fish hold, to do so would be dangerous, putting the boat in an unstable position. These were so vital that only the Captain or the chief engineer were allowed to touch these valves. There could be only one reason that these had been opened. To Sink the Investor. As the second day reached its end, the investigators were making their way back to the main bulkhead when the discovered more human remains, part of a foot, and two leg bones, the search now would continue until all light was lost. They found additional body parts; some were just small fragments of bone, still important to the investigation.

When Miller and Stogsdill had finished with the stem to stern examination of the Investor it was late on the evening of September 11, they had found everything they thought they could find.

There is nothing like a gruesome murder to lure the media. Even while the troopers had been trying to investigate the crime scene, the media were everywhere, a constant battle between the Troop ers and the press. While the troopers were having lunch one day a boat arrived full of press, microphones, and video cameras. The Troopers found themselves on CNN.

As with any reporting of a crime such as this, the press was more than willing to fill in any blanks and distort the details. The most exaggerated of these was that the Coulthursts had been murdered exacution style. The evidence was to the contrary, Mark and Irene had been found collapsed on one another somewhere near the galley. The rest of the bodies had been found near the area which contained the sleeping quarters. The false reports were beginning to take their toll on the investigators, Stogsdill had complained about the reporting early on, he was still sifting through the rubble and reports began to appear. The press seemed to know about everything that was taking place in Craig. Details were on CNN before they had been given to his superiors.

Lieutenant John Shover, from the A unit in Anchorage was put in charge of the investigation; he immediately was forced to face the press and deny most of what had been reported about the actual murders. "Bizarre as this thing is," he said, "we still don't have a motive."

The Coulthurst family was devastated not only with the crime toward the family, but the rumors surrounding the murders, rumors such as, Mark Coulthurst has several thousand dollars on him at the time of the murders, not true, a family spokesman said, " Mark always took his payments by check". Another report stated that a crewmember had committed the murders, John Coulthurst Marks father denied this report, saying that "all the crew were friends, this would never happen".

If the press was guilty of jumping to conclusions, then they were not alone, the Investor case seem to have as many people speaking "officially" for it, than it did press reporting it. The State Troopers as well as Ketchikan district attorney Mary Ann Henry were reporting daily, sometimes their reports conflicted, which only added to the confusion. One example was when the spokesman for the Alaska State Troopers Paul Edscorn was asked if there were any suspects, Edscorn replied that the troopers "had some definite people in mind" he also stated that they had recovered additional evidence from the Investor and it was being sent to the FBI for analysis.

The very same day, Mary Ann Henry told the press that no suspects had been identified and no further evidence had been recovered. This conflict only fueled rumors and confusion. Thus started the saga of "Keystone Cops."

The investigators Kolivosky and McCoy had scoured Prince of Whales Island, they had talked with ticket takers and deckhands at the ferry terminal, they watched every person boarding the ferry to Ketchikan, they looked at past passenger manifests, still no one matching the sketchy description of the suspect. Still believing that one man had acted alone. Sue Domenowske, Paul Pages girlfriend provided a similar description a man in his late teens or early twenties with thin blonde or brown hair. She told the investigators that the man had offered her the skiff to go out to the fire, she offered that the man seemed "like he wasn't very bright, or was in shock." She also stated that he didn't look like anyone she had ever seen in town."

Another witness was the owner of Craig Auto, the only gas station in Craig. The witness told the Troopers that a man had walked up with a gas can and bought some gas, not sure if it was Monday, the day before the fire. "A real decent type" the station owner related. He also said that the guy was wearing a baseball cap and "kind of a young guy", and might have been wearing glasses, other than that the station owner wasn't sure of anything more. McCoy and Kolivosky then tracked down someone they had talked to the day before, a man who had seen John Peel at the Libby 8 and said he knew him. They wanted to know exactly what the man had seen. The man again told them that his skiff had been only yards away from each other as they passed on the way to the fire. He again said that the man returning from the fire had light blonde hair, was wearing glasses and a baseball cap, he maybe had facial hair.

McCoy and Kolivosky knew that time was not on their side, memories were fading and descriptions were changing. They had to find this ghost and find him soon. The troopers kept looking for witnesses, another was found that claimed to have seen the Investor skiff on Tuesday at two o'clock, more than two hours before the fire. The skiff operator, he said, "was a middle aged man, probably native, medium height and stocky." Again another description, and another dead end.

The troopers headed back to Klawock, a meeting was scheduled to be held at Trooper Andersons house to review any and all material that had been gathered. Everyone would be there. At the end of the meeting it was hoped that a plan for finding and arresting the perpetrator would be formed. Attending the meeting were Captain Kolivosky, Lieutenant McCoy, Sergeants Stogsdill, Miller and Meek. Trooper Anderson. They were joined by Mary Ann Henry. There was plenty to be covered and the meeting lasted well into the night.

During the meeting they summarized the events as they knew them. The three bodies had been identified as Mark Coulthurst, his wife Irene and their daughter Kimberly. They knew that over 125 boats had been moored in or around Craig during the weekend of the murders. They also knew that the Investor had been tied up next to two other boats on the northern end of the float at North Cove. They knew she had arrived Sunday morning September 5th. They also knew she was seen leaving North Cove early on Monday September 6th.

They also knew that when the Investor left the float at North Cove she had left her lines behind, unusual because the lines were always undone from the float side and then tossed aboard the vessel. This showed that someone had been in a hurry and acting alone. Any attempts to contact the Investor that day were never answered; one boat tried to contact the Investor regarding her tie lines and had gotten no response. Despite the bad weather, several boats had noticed the investor anchored out in Ben's Cove all day Monday. No activity was seen aboard the boat as it lay at anchor.

Autopsy results showed that the Coulthursts were dead before the fire started. Alcohol tests revealed that most of the victims were drunk when they were killed. Pathology reports had estimated that there were only seven bodies, leading the troopers to believe that at least one crewmember was missing, and possibly the killer.

Tensions born out of frustration were mounting, Kolivosky and McCoy had turned up nothing, more had to be done. Composite sketches of the suspect hadn't been completed; nothing had been handed out around Craig. The residents of Craig were becoming very nervous. Everybody was pointing at everybody else, rumors were flying and the Press wasn't making it any easier. They needed a quick arrest, they needed to find the killers.

As the meeting wore on, Millers frustration was becoming more apparent, the case was not right from the beginning; he felt this from the moment he arrived in Craig. He had kept quiet, he sensed they had lost control early and the momentum was quickly dying. He was no longer able to keep his feelings to himself.

Anderson noticed that egos were starting to get in the way; Kolivosky and Miller were at odds. Anderson was becoming very uncomfortable; being the low man on the ladder he couldn't just call the meeting to a halt, even though it was taking place in his home. The meeting came to an abrupt end when Miller exploded. The target of his wrath was Kolivosky. "Either I'm going to be in charge, or you're going to be in charge, "he told the Captain. "And if you're going to be in charge, then I'm packing."

Miller's outburst made for even more tension in the meeting, but Kolivosky was not about to relinquish his control over the case to the CIB. The decision of who would have final jurisdiction over this case would have to be made in Anchorage.

The decision would come down Sunday morning. The Criminal Investigation Bureau would handle the Investor murders, the decision stated that the case required full-time investigators who had experience in such crimes. The investigation of the scene seemed to justify this decision. In Anchorage it seemed that Captain Kolivosky wanted off this case. Within months Kolivosky had another job, being well connected politically, he was appointed Commander of the State Troopers when Alaska elected a new governor, and this made Kolivosky the highest ranking trooper in the state.

Sergeant Miller was now the chief investigator, Stogsdill was his second in command. It was assumed that each man had his own expertise.

Miller had been a trooper for over fifteen years; he had served all over Alaska. He had been with the CIB since 1973. His expertise was homicide. Miller was a foreboding sight, black hair and a bushy mustache, he was not known for a sense of humor and what he did have was not always subtle. He had been known to wear a cap that had the words "Death Feeds My Family" on the front side. Miller was a family man, albeit somewhat unorthodox. He had investigated murders by professional hit men, also a contract killing by a motorcycle gang out of Anchorage.

Sergeant Stogsdill was also a family man. His demeanor was easy going and it was said he had a great sense of humor. A type-A personality, served in the military, came straight from the Air Force where he served as military policeman. He had already served ten years with the troopers and could retire in ten more. He had been assigned to the CIB in 1981, at which time he was promoted to sergeant.

The troopers decided to make Stogsdill an arson investigator, sending him to arson school in Chicago. This was followed by two weeks of on the job training. The Investor fire was the first major arson case he would work, baptism by fire you might say.

The two troopers knew that they would have to play catch up. Little did they realize they had more than a little catching up to do? It was like starting from scratch. Miller knew very little, almost nothing of the details from McCoy's interviews; they hadn't even read the notes that were taken by McCoy. So before they could figure out where the investigation was headed they would have to decipher where it had been. Miller and Stogsdill knew that anyone of interest had probably left Craig. The fishing season had ended and no one had any reason to stay. The two troopers headed to Petersburg, Alaska, 90 miles northeast of Craig.

In Petersburg they talked to three fishermen whose boats had been tied up next to the Investor in Craig. One of them said he had gathered the tie lines of the Investor which had been left on his boat. These lines had already been sent to the FBI to be fingerprinted; again Stogsdill and Miller were playing catch up.

All three fishermen told similar stories, they had all been very drunk that evening, they had awakened in time to see the Investor drifting away from the dock; they recalled the Investor drifted just a short ways then powered up and was gone. They agreed to that a lone figure was seen in the wheelhouse. Only one fisherman had any additional information. He said that Mark Coulthurst had asked to borrow $100.00, cash for which Coulthurst gave him a check. The fisherman said he didn't think twice about giving Coulthurst the money, "I trusted Mark," the fisherman said. The fisherman said he had seen the skiff from the

Investor tied up at the cold storage dock around 1:30 in the afternoon on Monday.

Miller and Stogsdill also learned that Coulthurst may not have had a large sum of cash aboard the Investor as some had thought. He had to borrow a lousy hundred bucks for his birthday dinner. This didn't seem important at the time, but would prove to have a great significance later.

Miller and Stogsdill also concluded that the crew of the Investor had been dead before they left the dock, that deduction was made from the fishermen's recalling seeing only one person aboard the Investor as she slipped away from the dock. The question the troopers were wrestling with now was, how could one person subdue the whole crew? Was there more than one killer? And if so, why? This all seemed like a dream, nothing seemed to fit.

Another piece of information was defiantly strange, one witness had seen the Investor's skiff in Craig at I;30, which led them to believe that the killer or killers, had returned to town before the fire. That meant that he or they would have had to return to the Investor to set her on fire then return to town once more. Somebody must have seen this man or men, somebody must remember something.

On Friday September 17th the day before the memorial service, the troopers who had traveled to Bellingham took time to travel north to the boarder town of Blaine, Washington. Blaine is where the Investor called home, a small town just a mile from the Canadian border. There they met with a former crewmember named LeRoy Flammang. Flammang had left the Investor just a week before the murders, coincidence, Or just luck. Flammang told Miller and Stogsdill what he could remember; the most important was where the crew had slept aboard the boat.

He remembered that the little girl and her mother shared one of the two bunks in the stateroom. The little boy slept in the day bed that was just of the wheelhouse. Flammang said that Johnny like to be near his dad, that information held significant importance, for if that was the case, it's very likely that the little boys body was totally consumed by the fire. The wheel house had been the hardest hit by the inferno.

Flammang went on to say that the rest of the crew had slept forward in the Investor, it was very narrow and the bunks were stacked two high very close to each other. Flammang did his best to recall exactly where each crew had slept; he said that Dean Moon was in the lower bunk on the starboard side. Mike Stewart had been on the top bunk over Dean Moon. That information fit, because Stewerts body had been recovered on the starboard side. Flammang said that Chris Heyman had been on the port side, the area that Flammang said he had slept on when he was aboard. This also seemed to be correct, the evidence that was believed to be the remains of Heyman were found on the portside of the boat, although it was just a few bones, a watchband and one molar tooth, the troopers felt that they were edging closer to identifying the crewmen.

Flammang was a retired Customs Officer, and had been on board the Investor for the 1982 season. Miller and Stogsdill asked Flammang if he had ever seen drugs on board the Investor, they prefaced the question by telling Flammang that the violence that appeared to have taken place aboard was hard to ignore, maybe a drug deal gone bad.

Flammang was less that forthcoming with answers about drugs on board, maybe due to his former position, maybe due to knowledge he was afraid to give, either way he just said "The kids were careful not to use around me."

Sergeant Miller asked Flammang "Was there anything we should know about your leaving the Investor when you did?" Flammang stated "I was tired. You know, I'm getting up in years and there was some irritation on board. I was ready to come home." Flammang didn't go into any detail about what may have been irritating him.

Miller found the statement to be disturbing, "an irritation on board" seemed important.

After the memorial Service on September 18th in Bellingham, Miller and Strogsdill reviewed the list of people they wanted to talk to. It seemed like everyone that had made the list worked aboard the Libby 8. All of them had been in Craig at the time of the murders. Dawn Holstrom made the list because of her contacts with the Investor crewmembers the night before the murders. Larry Demmert was on the list because he was the Captain of the Libby 8. John Peel made the list because he had known the Coulthursts and many of the Invertors crew.

John Peel was the only person on the list that the detectives could find. Peel met the troopers at the Holliday Inn in Bellingham. Accompanied by his wife Cathy, Peel agreed to answer any questions the troopers had. Seargent Miller noticed that the Peels seemed a bit nervous. The interview began with the usual questions, vital statistics, height, weight, date of birth. Peel said he weighed about 150lbs, was about five feet ten inches tall.

Miller told Peel that he just wanted to know what he could tell them about the crew on the Investor. They asked Peel if he knew of any of the activities on Sunday September 5th. Peel wasn't much help. Sensing the interview wasn't going to reveal much, Miller gave John Peel his business card. Miller told him to call if he could remember anything else.

As John Peel and his wife left the room, Sergeant Miller had a bad feeling, something didn't feel right. Although Peel hadn't said anything to draw suspicion to himself, his wife Cathy seemed to be a little to nervous, as the interview had gone on she became even more nervous. Why had she come? Why was it so important for her to be there? After all John Peel wasn't a suspect, Captain Kolivosky and McCoy had already eliminated him. Miller just had that feeling, something wasn't right. Why had John Peel been eliminated so soon as a suspect?

With John Peel eliminated early, the consensus was that the murders were done by a crewmember. The latest identification of remains was those of Jerome Keown, his body had been found on the stairs leading up to the galley. Reports showed that he had been shot in the arm, it may have been a defensive wound, and Keown may have been trying to raise his arm in defense.

With this identification it left only three bodies unidentified. Johnny Coulthurst only four years old was ruled out as the killer. Two crewmembers. Chris Heyman. And Dean Moon had not been identified. Not only that, the coroner now thought that only six bodies had been found on the Investor.

If that is the case, and one unidentified body was that of an adult male, the small boy was unaccounted for. It still held true that the fire was so intense in the area that the little boy was known to sleep, that his body could have been reduced to ashes and those ashes could have been washed away with the effort to extinguish the fire with the huge downpour of water that was dumped on the burning coffin. With this theory it was possible that one crewmember had survived the fire, this would have been either Chris Heyman or Dean Moon. This person would have to be a prime suspect.

John and Sally Coulthust adamantly denied that the killer of their son, pregnant daughter-in-law and grandchildren had been a crewmember of the Investor. They knew this just wasn't true.

It's now August 1983, a little over a year since the murders aboard the Investor. Still no real suspects, thousands of phone calls, hundreds of leads and no answers. Troopers have been all over the Alaska panhandle, traveling back and forth to Washington State so many times that the flight attendants knew them by their first names. All of this effort and still no one in custody.

The original investigators had been reassigned and now out of nowhere, these investigators were being re-assigned. It almost appeared that the case wasn't a priority anymore.

Sergeant Miller was transferred out of homicide and into state narcotics. Sergeant Stogsdill was transferred out of statewide narcotics and into homicide, this didn't seem strange at the time, but as I discovered later this was a calculated move.

The Investor case had been the most frustrating case of Sergeant Chuck Miller career. Soon after taking over the Investor case he realized that the witnesses seemed totally out of touch, their stories changed like the weather in Alaska, many of them had been drunk or loaded or both. Miller remembered that they started out ok, but then the stories just "got really flaky."

Miller decided that before he would hand over the case he wanted to hold a meeting. He called in almost twenty investigators from the Criminal Investigation Bureau. He called in Sergeant Holland from Seattle, and Detective McNeil from Bellingham.

Miller wanted everyone to go over everything "just one more time." They came from all directions, all converging on Ketchikan. There were Sergeants Stogsdill and Flothe, and Trooper Bullington, from Anchorage, Sergeant Iraelson from Petersburg. Trooper Anderson from Klawock. Sergeant Demmert from Fish & Wildlife. Sergeant Holland came in from Seattle and Sergeant Glass from Ketchikan. This would be known as the anniversary meeting.

As Miller had suggested, they would go over every lead, every bit of evidence, and every interview. The troopers started a "suspect list" one of the first to make the list was Dean Moon. His body was never identified from the debris of bones found in the burned out hull of the Investor. Crewmember Chris Heyman was the second to make the list for the exact same reason. Then there was John Glen Charles a native Alaskan who was experienced enough to have operated the skiff, and seemed to know a lot too much about the murders. He had been found dead just weeks after the murders. His death was ruled suicide.

Several others made the list, but it just appeared the troopers were reaching for the stars. Dean Moon wasn't ruled out completely, there had been a report that Dean Moon had been seen around fisherman's wharf in San Francisco, in fact an investigator was sent to the bay area to follow up on this report, again a dead end.

Someone had come forward and implicated Dean Moon and drugs aboard the Investor. Dean Moon was "heavy into drugs" the kind of drugs and the quantities that could get you killed.

The informant, who had contacted Miller in April of 1983, told Miller that Dean Moon had "ripped someone off for $20.000 or $30.000 in cocaine money." He also had been accused of stealing a large amount of marijuana from a grower in 1980. Again the drug angle was brought to light but the troopers just dismissed it as rumor.

Dean Moon's friends and family denied any notion that Moon had been involved in any more drug use than an occasional marijuana party.

John Peel presented a whole different set of problems for the investigation. Jerry Mackie who had strong feelings after seeing Peel at the Hill Bar the day after the fire was unable to produce any witnesses that could positively identify Peel. Plus Dawn Holstrom had provided Peel with an alibi; she told Sergeant Miller she had been with John Peel the day of fire. With that aside the troopers decided that John Peel needed to be put near the top of the list.

Even with the list of suspects narrowing the troopers were not ruling out the possibility that someone not on their list, someone not even on the radar had committed the murders. The rumor of a "contract killing or a mob hit" was still in the back of some of the troopers minds. The feeling among most of the investigators was still pointing to someone who had been in the area of the Investor at the time of the killings. There had been four boats around the Investor on the night of the murders. The boats were the Decade, the Defiant, the Cindy Sue and the Libby 8. The troopers thought that if they could find which of these crewmembers had been with the crew of the Investor they might have a chance to identify the killer. In order to do this they would have to find and interview fishermen who had been in Craig the previous season, no easy task for this season was running out. The fishermen would scatter once again.

On August 29th Trooper Anderson found the Libby 8 tied up in Craig. Stogsdill and Flothe arrived on Prince Of Wales Island and immediately headed to the Libby 8. She was an old wooden boat built sometime in the 1940's. She belonged to the cannery and was leased out to fish. She was defiantly not the Investor. The first crewman from the Libby 8 to be interviewed was Brian Polinkus who had been on the Libby 8 the summer of the murders and was also aboard this season. Polinkus provided some insight as how the paths of the Investor and the Libby 8 had become interwoven the summer before, a strange tale indeed.

Polinkus stated that John Peel had brought Jerome Keown and Dean Moon on board the Libby 8 the night before the murders. They only stayed a few minutes. Polinkus thought it might have been around three or four o'clock in the afternoon. He said they didn't talk about much, he did remember the talk was centered around Irene Coulthurst who wasn't real happy about having the kids on the boat. She wanted to leave the next day, I think she had made plans, Polinkus said.

The Troopers needed more; Flothe asked Polinkus if Dean Moon had a friend on the Libby 8 who would that have been? Polinkus answered without hesitation, "John Peel, he was the only guy; he had introduced them to me." Polinkus was asked if there had been guns on board the Libby 8, he said that the skipper Larry Demmert had a .22 long rifle and John Peel had a 30.30. Speaking with Larry Demmert added some more details. He told troopers he'd noticed the investors skiff tied up at the cold storage dock, his information was key because he said it was on the morning before the fire. Demmert also said that

John Peel and Dawn Holstrom were good friends with Dean Moon and Jerome Keown, this contradicted Polikus.

Demmert went on to say that the bunch of them were on the Libby 8 drinking beer and just hanging around the Sunday before the fire. Demmert also noted that around ten-thirty that evening he returned from town and saw people aboard the Investor, it looked like a party Demmert said. Flothe asked Demmert if anyone was on board the Libby 8 when he returned. "Nobody" Demmert replied. "Just me."

When the troopers were finished with Larry Demmert they had a very bad feeling about John Peel. When Demmert had insisted he was alone on the Libby 8 the night before the murders, they remembered John Peel had said something different, he said he had been on the Libby 8 that night. That he'd come home early and gone to sleep. Either Larry Demmert had been wrong or John Peel was lying.

Demmert told him that there had been a five gallon gas can aboard the Libby 8. The troopers knew that the killer had carried such a can when he torched the Investor. Demmert said the can was still on board the boat when they had unloaded and the can was still full. Demmert also said that he did have a .22 rifle but he always kept it locked up in his stateroom.

Larry Demmerts girlfriend had said earlier that she was with Dawn Holstrom and John Peel when they had noticed the fires. But when she was questioned again she said it may not have been John Peel but instead it may have been Brian Polinkus.

John Peel's alibis seemed to be melting away. The problem as the troopers saw it was that it was ones persons word against the other. Time had taken its toll on memories.

The interviews were about over, and again nothing concrete had been found, the suspect list had been narrowed, some had fallen off, some had been moved up, still no one had been arrested.

It was now November, 1983. After the interviews in August the investigation seemed to narrow considerably. Rumors of Dean Moon's drug dealing were never verified. The informant was found to be less than creditable; in fact he had lied about even knowing Dean Moon.

On November 4th Sergeant Stogsdill received a letter from Arcata, California. The letter was from a grad student who had been fishing in Alaska at the time of the murders. The letter said that the student had read an article about the unsolved homicides in the October, 1983, issue of the Alaska Fisherman's Journal.

He said that having seen the composite sketches in the article, something had clicked. He had seen someone that resembling the composites. He said he had seen him in the Investor skiff as he made a power landing at the cold storage dock.

He said it was around ten o'clock on Monday morning, it was Labor Day. The day before the fire. He said he also had encountered the Investor's crew, he had run into them at the laundromat on Sunday night. He said they looked tired and had beards, they were smoking pot. Stogsdill called Joe Weiss. After talking to Weiss, Stogsdill decided to fly to California. Hoping this wasn't another wild goose chase.

In California, Stogsdill showed Weiss two books of photos. The first book contained a photo lineup of six pictures all head shots. In this lineup was a picture of John Peel. Stogsdill asked Weiss "if you were to have to pick someone out of this lineup, which one would you choose?" Stogsdill asked.

Weiss said if he had to pick one it would be number three, he's the one who looks most like the person I saw. Weiss didn't hesitate; he liked the color and length of the hair. He liked the bone structure of the face.

Number three was John Peel. Weiss said that the pictures were not real good, "really fuzzy". Stogsdill moved on to the next book of photos, this book contained picture of the Investor crewmembers. Stogsdill hoped that Weiss could identify the crewmembers he had seen at the Craig Laundromat. He did recognize several photos. They were photos of Jerome Keown and Dean Moon. He wasn't so sure this time. "I just remember they hadn't shaved and had dark hair" Weiss said.

After interviewing Weiss, Stogsdill decided to fly to Bellingham instead of returning to Alaska. He wanted to meet with the Coulthurst family. When he arrived in Bellingham the Coulthurst were planning the wedding for their youngest daughter Lisa. There was so much to do, Marilyn Peel; John Peel's mother was baking the wedding cake.

Stogsdill had some questions to ask the Coulthurst's. The Coulthurst had the answers. John Coulthurst the patriarch of the family told Stogsdill that Mark had met John Peel through his daughter Lisa, who had dated John Peel for some time. Mark Coulthurst had offered John Peel a job right here in this living room the elder Coulthurst said.

Peel had worked for Mark for two seasons on the Kit, the elder Coulthurst said, and this was the first boat that Mark had. It was a purse seiner, the boat Mark Coulthurst had before the Investor. John Coulthurst said that during the 1981 John Peel was fired. He was late for work, he was stoned and he was drunk on the job. Mark had no choice but to let him go. Fishing is dangerous enough without those distractions John Coulthuurst stated. When Marks mother, Sally Coulthurst spoke, she could barely contain herself. She remembered telling Sergeant Miller about the composites back in 1982. She pointed to the same one that Joe Weiss had picked out, telling Miller that looks like "John Peel." Miller had just ignored her. Stogsdill was open to anything at this time that might help. Sally Coulthurst had one more thing she needed to tell Sergeant Stogsdill. She had learned that John Peel had sold some dope to Moon and Keown on Sunday, September 5th, the night before the murders. She told Stogsdill the last time she saw John Peel she confronted him. She told Peel "You know something that you haven't told the troopers," "Next time they're in town, you better tell them."

Sergeant Stogsdill wanted to interview Peel again, after the meeting with the Coulthurst he had many more questions for Mr. Peel. Stogsdill and Sergeant Roy Holland arrived at Peel's place of employment. Peel was working for a company that made floats for marinas. Peel agreed to talk with them; he suggested they meet at a bar so he could have a beer that idea didn't go over very well. Stogsdill told Peel to meet them at the police station.

John Peel arrived at the Police Station after work, around four-thirty. Stogsdill noticed that Peel was wearing a halibut jacket and a baseball cap. Peel was put in an interview room that had a two way mirror. This served two purposes, one for the interview and the other allowed them to take additional photos of John Peel.

This interview would turn out to be more important than Stogsdill and Holland first had thought. Stogsdill asked Peel about the allegations of drug dealing that Mark Coulthursts mother had told them about earlier. Peel said that he had sold some marijuana to some of the investor crew. Peel denied that he sold any other drugs to anyone else. Once Peel started talking freely, the questions started bombarding him from the investigators. Asked how he had arrived in Alaska that summer, Peel replied that he had hitched a ride on the boat called the Cleveland. He said when he reached Ketchikan that he saw Mark Coulthurst and asked him for a ride to Craig. Coulthurst told him he wasn't going to Craig. Peel said he had to pawn his watch to raise enough money to take the ferry to Hollis. Upon arriving in Craig he noticed the Investor tied up in North Cove.

The next question Stogsdill asked Peel was about the Investor fire. Peel said he had gone out on the Cindy Sue while the Investor was burning. "How big was the fire when you got to it?" Stogsdill asked.

Peel responded that "all the bulwarks were burned back." He was describing the raised area around the deck of the boat. Stogsdill knew that he had caught Peel in the first of what would be many lies. The bulwarks hadn't burned at all.

"What else did you do that day?" Stogsdill asked.

"I called my parents," Peel replied.

At this point the troopers showed Peel some photographs, he asked Peel about these composites of the skiff man, and Stogsdill asked Peel if he had ever seen these before.

"Yeah," Peel replied. "They didn't do a thing for me." Peel responded that the composites "reminded me of Larry Demmert, Jr."

Stogsdill asked Peel if he had any thoughts about the murders, asking him about the rumors of a big drug deal gone bad. Peel didn't respond.

By the time the interview was over and Peel had left the Bellingham Police Station, Stogsdill was suspicious and had come to a conclusion. Stogsdill and Holland knew that John Peel was number one on their suspect list.

How could one man have killed all those people? How could one man overtake eight people? How was it possible that none of the crewmembers weren't able to fight back, after all they were young strong fishermen. Could it be because there was more than one Killer?

In Bellingham. Detective McNeil had managed to contact Larry Demmert, Jr. A few months earlier Mr. Demmert had turned over a .22 caliber rifle that had been on the Libby 8. A crewmember had also brought in the same caliber rifle that had been on the Libby 8 the previous season. Detectives were hoping that one of these could be the murder weapon; also they were looking to link John Peel to one of these rifles.

Larry Demmert, Jr. was also able to provide further information. Demmert told Stogsdill, he saw someone on the dock who seemed to match the description of the skiff operator. Demmert said that he had never seen this person before. He also told the detectives that he remembered waking up about 2:00 am. Monday morning. He said he just felt something wasn't right. He didn't think anyone else was aboard the Libby 8 he hadn't heard anyone come aboard. Months earlier Demmert had called the Bellingham police and told them that he had woken up to "something strange." "I felt evil in the air" Demmert told the police. The information wasn't deemed important so it was never passed along.

Demmert also told detective Stogsdill, on the day of the fire he had made one trip out to the Investor, he had used his father's boat for the trip, and John Peel did not come along. Demmert told Stogsdill that Peel said" I don't feel like going out to the fire." Demmert said Peel went to get a beer.

Almost everyone who had been shown the composites in the last few months have pointed to John Peel, sometimes not positive identifications, but close enough. With all these witnesses, pointing to John Peel, the Troopers were now going to confront John Peel with the evidence.

Stogsdill had called the Bellingham Herald the local newspaper. Stories of the Investor murders had filled the pages. Stogsdill also made arrangements for the local television station KVOS to broadcast some of the film that the troopers had produced showing the burning Investor. They also agreed to show the entire film later in the week. Associated Press had picked up the story. "It was everywhere" one of the locals recalled. Turning up the pressure, Stogsdill had put out a formal statement requesting anyone who had any information to come forward.

On Tuesday, March 20th. The Herald ran a front page story written by staff writer Donald Tapperson. The article said that four Alaska State Troopers had arrived in town, "to pursue their continuing investigation of the mass murder aboard the fishing boat Investor..." "We're not letting up," the article quoted Sergeant Stogsdill.

On Wednesday, March 21st. The Herald ran another story prodded by Stogsdill. The headline read "Police uncover new witness in the Investor case." The article went on to say that a "new witness had emerged in the mass murder aboard the Investor". It also reported that "with fresh information that has given the Alaska State Troopers new hope for a solution. " The recent development of highly detailed 'behavioral' and 'abilities' profiles of the wanted man, coupled with the speculations about his motive for the crimes, has led the team's leader, Sergeant Stogsdill, to believe that "we're on the way to the end. A solution is closer than before."

In a related piece, Stogsdill provided a detailed description of their suspect. This was done with the hope of flooding the phones with people pointing fingers. Stogsdill described their suspect as a white male, in his late teens or early twenties. A fisherman. Stogsdill was also very careful to add information that would point directly to John Peel. Adding fuel to the fire, Stogsdill noted that the suspect was believed to have been a crewman on another boat at the time of the murders. He would have a place to go after the killings. That he knew some of the crew of the Investor, maybe even partied aboard the Investor the night of the murder. The full court press was on and John Peel was the only player on the court.

Almost two tears had passed since the murders aboard the Investor. In May of 1984, the homicide unit of the Criminal Investigation Bureau was disbanded. Most all of the officers were sent into the bush, the case loads that the troopers were working were handed over or closed.

Sergent Stogsdill was sent to the Kenai Peninsula. He was stationed in the small town of Soldotna, population 2000, a far cry from Anchorage with its 180,000 people. He also went from a Homicide detective to a general Investigator. His job derscription was solve everything. The Kenai is south of Anchorage and had several small villages. It has a total of nearly 1200 miles and extends all the way to the tip of the Aleutian Islands. When Stogsdill arrived he inherited a real mess. A double homicide in Egegik. In Dillingham he had a rape case, as well as several internal affairs investigations involving local police and State Troopers. Stogsdill was told that he could keep the Investor case, however he knew that due to his location it would be almost impossible to do any real work on the Investor murders. His biggest fear was that this would become just another cold case.

In July of 1984, Stogsdill met with Roy Holland to review all the statements that had been taken regarding the Investor, the last time this was done was in the summer of 1983. Many new witnesses had been interviewed since then and there was always a chance that something had been said, maybe a clue, maybe a small bit of overlooked information, anything that might give Stogsdill renewed hope.

When the two of them finished their review, they realized that John Peel had been lying every step of the way during the investigation. Although the evidence was circumstantial, it was piling up in massive amounts.

The listed the facts, Peel knew the Coulthursts, he was seen with the Investor crew the night before the murders, and he can't account for his whereabouts for about three days surrounding the murders. Witnesses had seen someone that resembled Peel in the Investors skiff. The same witnesses had seen Peel on two separate days, Monday and Tuesday. This was all the troopers had, except for a very strange report about Larry Demmert Jr. Demmert had been asked to bring some ammunition in so the FBI could do some ballistic analysis, to check against the bullets taken from the bodies. Demmert delievered the ammunition, not to the police station however. Demmert insisted that they meet somewhere else to make the hand off. When Troopers suggested that they just come to Demmerts home and pick up the ammo, Demmert insisted that they never come to his house; he said he didn't want any police near his home. The exchange went down at Clark Market on James street in Bellingham. Demmert told the troopers that he was afraid his home was being watched and he felt he was in danger.

Any physical evidence by this time, almost two years after the murders, wasn't going to be any better than it was at the time of the killings. The forensic evidence, such as the bone fragments, the teeth and whatever else was there was just gathering dust in the evidence room in Anchorage. Possibly one day science would be able to open new areas and provide the key that would unlock the mystery. The evidence room held all of the evidence, anything and everything else had been consumed by the fire aboard the Investor.

Business As Usual

In the early 1970's Anchorage was a hub of activity of all sorts. The money that was flowing in from the Trans Alaskan pipeline was abundant, all sorts of commerce was flourishing. Business was booming and long time family business were no exception. A family business that was started by a matriarch was no exception, however this business was different, and this business was drug dealing. Drugs were flooding the pipeline; cocaine was "everywhere" according to Alaska State Troopers. The area is so vast and we are spread so thin, that enforcement is all but non existent. Knowing this, drug dealers were almost free to do anything the wanted anywhere they wanted.

The head of this family was a small petite woman in her mid thirties, non assuming and very careful in her daily routines. Her base of operation was out of a bar she owned, this bar was frequented by construction workers, fishermen and of course workers coming in from the pipeline with pockets full of cash. She started out small being very selective as to who would be able to purchase from her.

She eventually started to move larger quantities, all of her clients came recommended from a client she already knew and had dealt with. Her business allowed her to live a lavish lifestyle and her fortune grew until the day she decided she wanted to leave Alaska.

Taking over the family business was her 20 year old son; he had watched and learned at "his mother's knee". He started making local deliveries for his mother when he was aged 10; he had become street wise and low key. His appearance was normal, small but stocky build, light brown hair, sometimes he would wear glasses other times just regular non assuming clothing. His home was in a modest suburb of Anchorage called Stuckagain heights; he had a live in Girlfriend and was raising her 6 year old son. His girlfriend worked for the airlines that bears the State name. Outside appearances was that of a hard working guy taking care of his family.

Once he had control of the family business, he sought to expand, reach out; this was done with calculated precision. His contacts had become invaluable, many held high positions, some in Law Enforcement, some in the legal system, and one in particular was a union leader. He was the most valuable, for he controlled the pipeline, and the pipeline was where the money was.

Part of his success was his ability to fit in, never flashy, always maintained the same daily routine. His day began every morning a 6am; he got up fixed breakfast, walked his dog, got into his older pick-up truck and left his residence. Nothing out of the ordinary, the same thing was happening all over Anchorage everyday. Construction was booming so he attracted no attention from anyone. Just routine. He kept a separate residence for his business, a small broken down trailer in Spenard, the area of Anchorage that for years contained many "red light" districts. During the construction of the Trans Alaska Pipeline, Spenard had unprecedented growth of bars, night clubs and other disreputable business. These businesses catered to the fat wallets of those coming down fro the North Slope for rest and relaxation. The other side of his life was a different story, wise well beyond his years he had begun moving large quantities of cocaine from the "Lower 48". He had connections from Florida to California, from Columbia to Mexico, getting his product was no problem, getting it into Alaska presented more of a challenge.

In the 1970's and 1980's the airlines were still an option, smaller quantities were easily stored in luggage and checked thru to destinations all over Alaska. For larger quantities bigger containers had to be found, and he found them. Commercial fishing vessels left to fish the Alaska waters from all ports, some from as far as California and some as close as the towns near the Canadian border. Two of these towns were Bellingham Washington and Blaine Washington, both near the border and both a four or five day run up the inside passage to Alaska. Along this route were several small towns and villages that made unloading his cocaine easy and thousands of small islands made detection almost imposable. Finding willing fishing boats was not hard; finding willing crew members was even easier. Most were clients and more than willing to trade drugs for moving his loads. At the peak he was moving fifty kilos or more than 120 lbs of cocaine a month. Cocaine was going for $30.000 to $40

.000 per kilo or 2.2lbs. Once it reached Alaska it would sell for $20.000 per pound, broken down it would bring even more. He had now become one of the largest drug dealers in Alaska. All while posing as a hard working construction worker.

As with any drug dealer, payment was sometimes taken in other forms, he was no different. In a warehouse in an industrial area on the outskirts of Anchorage he had stored several classic cars worth thousands dollars, polar bear skins, ivory, gold, boats, jewelry, as well as cash. This was his fort Knox. No one but he had any knowledge of this unit, it was rented under an assumed name and visited only by him.

THE PIPELINE

Construction began on the 798 mile long Trans Alaskan pipeline in April, 1974. Before the actual pipeline itself could be constructed, a road had to be built paralling the pipeline, it started from Livengood and ended in Deadhorse. It was the Dalton Highway later referred to as the "Haul Road "it was built to move massive loads of equipment, gasoline, and housing materials, for the estimated 70.000 men and women who would undertake such a gigantic undertaking. The newest Alaska rush is for oil. Recoverable oil, reserves on the North Slope had been estimated to be between somewhere from 10 billion to 30 billion gallons or maybe even more.

The pipeline and all subsequent construction which included the road had an estimated cost of $8 billion dollars. Over 2000 contractors and subcontractors would work on this from all parts of the "lower 48". They represented all areas of construction. Most were members of unions; they would arrive in Alaska check in with their local union houses and be sent north to work. The pay was well above anything that the lower 48 had to offer so once again "The Boom "was on. All sorts of people started heading north to seek their fortune, only this time the payment was assured. Work hard and long hours and pockets would be stuffed with cash. Money flowed long before oil.

A visitor to Alaska during this time would soon sense the gusto of pipeline activity. Airline schedules are tight and planes are full with businessmen from the "Lower 48" states. In Fairbanks or Anchorage the cab driver would usually ask what phase of the pipeline you were working on. If you were to ask anyone you might meet how long they had lived in Alaska the answer was more often than not "just a few months".

A hotel room could run anywhere from $36.00 to $200.00 depending on your needs or bankroll. Hamburgers were $3.00 and a one bedroom apartment should you be lucky enough to find one would run $1,200 or more.

Just as it was in the 1800's when gold was the oil of its day, the attraction was not only for hard working men and women, but all sorts of people that prayed upon the isolation and loneliness of these workers. It was nothing to see short skirted ladies of the night walking the streets in twenty degrees below zero temperatures cashing in on those fat pipeline checks. However unlike the "Gold Rush" days, there was another type of predator just waiting for the big money. Supplying the scarce but highly demanded drugs. Dealers and smugglers had found a "Gold Mine." Cocaine was the drug of choice for thousands. Working long hours sometimes not sleeping for 24 to 36 hours, they sought out anything to relieve any and all stresses, or just to keep them awake so the overtime money would boost the already fat checks.

Cocaine and other drugs were coming in from the "Lower 48". A kilo of good cocaine was going for $30,000. Broken down it would bring over $250.000. So dealers and smugglers were constantly finding new ways to transport their product. Some of it was coming in by plane, some by car and some by boat. The fishing industry provided thousands of opportunities for this type of delivery. Fishing boats coming from the "Lower 48" would provide an endless supply.

Like any other business the drug business along the pipeline had its higharchy, in order to gain access to the workers on the pipeline you had to know somebody or be somebody. The best place to start was the Union halls, if you could get the attention of someone who had control of who went to work and who didn't then your chances for moving your product was assured.

The Unions that worked the pipeline had a huge amount of power, so therefore the men who ran the union halls wielded untold authority and accessibility.

One of the largest Unions was the Labor union out of Anchorage Alaska. Anchorage was a large city with a population well over 200,000.

Growing by the day, surrounded by water on one side and beautiful mountains on the other. Anchorage had survived a large earthquake in the early sixties that devastated its downtown area as well as the bluffs south of town; many people were injured and killed. Like any other event in Alaska it seemed that the people remained strong and determined to rebuild. The downtown area now had high-rise hotels, beautiful wide streets and the rural areas had begun to flourish as the town started to spread put. Like any large town, Anchorage had its darker side.

Spenard was such a place, not far from downtown Spenard are many trailer parks, some with newer mobile homes but most contained rundown old trailers, as you drive down some of these streets you could see small add on shacks to the trailers, the broken down fences, the abandoned cars, and the history of this town lay in the streets. Spenard also was home to several bars and strip joints, on almost every street you would see "massage parlor" signs', some in neon, some just painted on the side of the building. This is where you could get almost anything you pocket book could afford. This was a good place to hide, or hide what you were doing, the police just tried to keep what went on there corralled to this area. A good place to fit in.

THE TRIAL I

As quaint and beautiful as Ketchikan is, the ugliest building in town is the State Office Building. The trial is taking place on the fourth floor of this cold non descriptive slab of concrete. As Larry and I approached he said "I hope it's better on the inside", I agreed, and we proceeded to walk thru the heavy metal doors. The media seemed like they were everywhere.

Ruth Moon the mother of one of the murdered crewmembers Dean Moon was overheard saying that this is nothing but a "circus", people had already started to gather on the fourth floor and the muffled noise was almost defining. The trial was scheduled to begin promptly at nine, it was already 9:30 and there was a dely. This would prove to be just the beginning in delays and confusion. No one wanted to be there, you could see the families standing together, not wanting to look at each other. These are families that once let their children play together, attended weddings together, watched their kids play sports, now torn apart, ripped to shreds. Larry stayed close to my side as if he was trying to hide, after all he was going to testify today against a childhood friend, against a family, and in his words "against my home town, my life will never be the same." John Coulthurst Sr. came over and Larry introduced me. Mr. Coulthurst was a large man, he had a deep voice, he told Larry to be strong and just tell the truth. Larry shook his hand, and the elder Coulthurst rejoined his family who were huddled by the door.

It was now almost 10:00am and the court doors opened, Larry couldn't come in as he was to be the first witness after opening arguments.

I said I'd see him later and I proceeded to push my way in. I found a seat two rows back on the isle just behind the defense table.

I got my first glance at the defendant John Peel, he was dressed in a long sleeve shirt covered by a stripped sweater, black slacks and appeared neatly groomed. Sitting beside him was his attorney Phillip Weidner. Weidner was dressed in what appeared to be a well worn suit, tied at the waist with a rope; he sported a long black beard and had an air of arrogance that I suppose he would need to defend his client. I later found out that Weidner had graduated from Harvard Law School, as had the District attorney Mary Anne Henry who would be the lead prosecutor. The stage was set.

I later found out that the delay in starting the trial was due to the attorneys arguing over who would sit where in the courtroom. Finally Judge Schulz made the decision as who would sit where. In the end he divided the courtroom like congress. He didn't want the two sides intermingling. The family of the victims would sit on the same side as the prosecution lawyers. John Peel's family would sit behind the defense table. The actual sitting arrangements would prove to be of little importance. The families of the murder victims were not going to be able to attend the entire trial due to financial restraints. However John Peel's family was able to rent a house in Ketchikan and stay the entire time. This is the same family that had to rely on friends to post the million dollar bail.

The courtroom was packed; near the jury box was a scale model of the Investor, and another model of Craig which included a scale model of the entire float as well as all the boats that were moored near or next to the investor, complete to the smallest detail, boat lines, light poles, dock carts and anything that would allow the jury to get a feel for the scene that gruesome night in Craig. These took up so much room that the attorneys had little room to roam.

As I was soon to find out, this trial was going to be a long tedious attempt to paint a picture of one man gone crazy. The prosecutor Mary Anne Henry opened the states argument by staring directly at John Peel. A large woman, with plain features, she seemed uncomfortable in heels and a dress. During her opening statement, she hardly moved in the courtroom. I could see her apparent nervousness, this was the biggest trial of her career, yet I found her less than intimidating. Having been on several juries, I always found the opening statements to carry the initial weight. Although judges tell juries that opening statements are not evidence, verdicts are eerily consistent with the jury's first impression, not only of who presents it but what is said during the statements.

One by one, she presented the names of each victim, Mark Coulthurst, Irene Coulthurst, daughter Kimberly age five, son John age 4, crewmembers Dean Moon, Jerome Keown, Mike Stewart, and Chris Heyman. All the while she stared at John Peel as if to try to convince the jury that there was no doubt who committed these horrendous crimes. Henry went on for several more minutes listing more names; it became apparent to me that this jury was in for a long tedious almost dizzying challenge of their memories. As I have stated before, serving on jury duty is never easy, if you have ever been in a pre-selection jury room, the conversations of the prospective jurors is very seldom positive, most of the conversations revolve around how much of a burden this will be, how can I get out of this and so on. My response was "if it was you, how would you like to be judged by someone with your attitude. That usually would end any conversation.

I could foresee the jurors in this case getting very weary by the time this was over.

⌐

Mary Anne Henry stated that everyone on her list had a part to play in this trial, she emphasized that everyone would play an important role as the trial proceeded. A total of 62 people had been named by the time she was done. This took more than three hours, three hours of tedious explanations. For three hours Mary Anne Henry presented evidence that pointed to John Peel.

As I sat there I looked around the small room, I could see different expressions on peoples faces, worried looks from Peels family, grief and sorrow from the victims families, shock on some jury members, and high expectations from the media.

I was waiting for Henry to present a motive for this gruesome crime- she did not mention one explicitly; she pointed to John Peel's resentment, the fact that he had not had a successful fishing season in 1982. He had been stuck on the Libby 8, Larry Demmert Jr. boat. A boat that had numerous break downs and his share of proceeds would only be five percent. His counterpart aboard the Investor would be getting twelve percent. This would have meant thousands of dollars. His counterpart was Dean Moon.

Henry went on to say that John Peel was seen staggering aboard the Investor. John Peel was seen on the dock holding a rifle, the screams that Larry had heard, the fact that Peel had gone missing until sometime during the day following the murders. Peel saying he was with his girlfriend, when he wasn't . Peel going missing again for two days after that.

She went on to describe how John Peel had taken the boat to Ben's Cove, opening the valves on the Investor so she would sink. She described Peel taking the Investors skiff and "leaving eight dead bodies on board a sinking ship, two of which were just little children".

She then went on to describe the next day, the day of the fire. She told the jury that the Investor hadn't sunk, as John Peel had planned. "John Peel went into town and made a phone call at 11:56 a.m. to a travel agency in Ketchikan. John Peel then went to the gas station, Jim Robinson's gas station in downtown Craig, and there he bought gas, the gas he used to burn the Investor and all the people that lay dead within its hull. He saturated the bodies with gasoline, and he lit them on fire. He then jumped back in the skiff and headed straight back to the cold storage dock.

She told the jury about people who saw John Peel in the skiff, about the unsuccessful attempts to put out the fire, about the discovery of the melted bodies that Trooper Anderson had found. She also showed a short jerky film of the Investor consumed in flame. She also described John Peel in Bellingham, a scene where John peel was confronted by police. Henry's description of Peel saying everything but the "magic words" I did it. John Peel didn't say I didn't do it, he didn't say he was innocent. John Peel didn't even get angry Henry said. All John Peel did was ask questions, trying to find out what the police knew, there was a definite anger in her tone.

She went on to say "There is no living person who witnessed those murders, except John Peel. The evidence that you are going to hear will be more than adequate to convict John Peel; the evidence will be beyond any reasonable doubt. John Peel on that night snapped, he went aboard the Investor and fired that first shot, Evidence will prove that John Peel went on to murder all of those people. At the end of this trial I will stand before you and ask that you hold John Peel responsible for what he did. With that Mary Anne Henry thanked the jury for their time, and told Judge Schulz that she finished with her opening statements. It had taken four and a half hours.

Judge Schulz asked if the defense was ready to proceed with their opening statements. To the courts surprise Defense attorney Phillip Weidner decided not to follow directly upon Mary Anne Henry's heels. Instead he requested that his opening be scheduled for tomorrow. "I want the jury to be fresh" Weidner stated. Judge Schulz agreed and Court was dismissed for the day. I waited in my seat as most everyone filed out. I wanted to look John Peel in his eyes, as he passed right by me. I stood as he approached, looked directly at his face, he had a smirk, a slight smile, he caught my stare, I noticed his smirk quickly disappear as he looked me directly in eye. I got the feeling that he knew that I knew and I had him puzzled. I saw his attorney glance my way and catch the brief scene that had taken place. Weidner wasn't sure what the glance had meant if anything, but I knew he was not going to let it go by.

I met with Larry outside the courtroom, he had all sorts of questions, and I put my arm around him and quickly escorted him outside. Again I noticed Weidner staring at the two of us. I felt the uneasy stare as Larry and I walked away from the courthouse.

There was still some daylight left as we left the courthouse, so I suggested that we walk back to the Motel. As we turned left and began walking toward the motel I felt that we weren't alone. As we walked along the sidewalk which bordered the small shops I was able to notice the reflection of someone following us in the shop windows. I didn't mention this to Larry; he was already a nervous wreck. The day had already proven that this trial wasn't going to be without its turmoil.

Once Larry and I had arrived at the Motel we spotted Larry's father in the lobby, not having eaten all day I asked both of them if they would like to join me for some dinner? Declining, they said that they just wanted to get some rest and spend some time together, so they left and I went into the coffee shop. As I was waiting to be seated I noticed a large man dressed in a black coat his head was covered with a hat that hid his face as he turned my way, spotting me he quickly turned and left through the double doors of the Motel entrance.

This just proved without a doubt that I was of some interest to someone here in Ketchikan, who I didn't know, but I was sure I would find out soon enough. Having finished dinner I returned to my room to relax and get some rest. Just as I was about to lay down the phone rang, it was Larry, he wanted to meet, and he said his father wanted to talk to me. Gathering myself together I said I would be right down. Arriving at Larry's room I noticed that his bags were packed. I asked him what the hell he was doing. he said his father wanted him to change rooms, he was getting the room that adjoined mine. Here I am looking at this strong, physical young man, all of a sudden he appears as a scared little boy. His father asked me if it would be ok if he moved closer to me, without hesitation I said sure, his father went on to explain that he was returning to Bellingham as soon as he had been called to testify and he was afraid for Larry. This was beginning to be much more than I had bargained for.

Getting Larry moved and settled in just took a few minutes, his father thanked me and returned to his room. Once in Larry's room I asked him "what's going on?" he stood silent for some time, then turned, as he did I could see he had been crying, again I asked the same question. His reply shocked me, "I think someone is following me, I don't know who it would be, but I feel someone doesn't want me to testify, I'm scared". I replied that I also have noticed someone who seems to be following me. I assured Larry that I would take care of this situation, that he is safe; I also told him that he should tell the State troopers, they would insure his safety. Larry replied "what if it's them? What if they think I'll fuck this up for them? I again reassured him that I would take care of this. In the back of my mind I wasn't sure what I could do, but I wasn't going to let Larry see my concern.

In a past life I had been on the other side of this scenario, I knew that I could at least call on some old tricks that might allow me to uncover what was going on. I said goodnight to Larry and went through the adjoing door that separated our rooms.

I placed a call home, reassuring my wife that all was well and that I would see her soon, again wishing her a happy birthday.

After hanging up the phone, I paced the floor, thinking of who I might call to get some help or at least some advice on this situation. After some searching my mind, I remembered a friend in Seattle, a man that at one time worked for an agency of the government that relied on their ability to work undetected in many areas. He and I had met in South America during the sixties. I think they're referred to as "Spooks". We had been friends for over twenty years; if anyone could help it would him. It was late, and I was tired so I decided to call him in the morning.

I didn't sleep well that night, I kept hearing Larry pacing and his television was on all night, just loud enough to make sleeping almost impossible.

Larry and I met in the coffee shop at 7:30 a.m., we ate a light breakfast. We discussed the day ahead of us and I told Larry that the defense was going to start their opening statements this morning and I didn't foresee him getting to the stand before lunch. I told him we would meet for lunch and go from there. I suggested that he take a taxi with his father to the courthouse and I would follow later. I wanted time to call my friend.

Larry and his father left for the courthouse about 8:15, I returned to my room to make the call. Something stopped me just as I picked up the receiver to place the call. The thought crossed my mind that my room phone may be compromised; I needed to make the call from an outside line. I finished dressing, made sure my room was in order, put the do not disturb sign on the outside door handle and proceeded to begin walking to the courthouse. I remembered there was a bank of pay phones just outside the courtroom on the fourth floor. I arrived at the cement palace around 8:45, the crowd had already gathered, same faces, same stares. We were notified that the doors would open at 9:30 due to motions being made by the attorneys. This would give me a chance to make my call.

The phone rang several times before being answered. After some time talking pleasantries, I made my case. My friend asked some questions, and the conversation was over. It was just a few minutes and the doors to the courtroom opened, this time I wasn't the first one in. I looked around for a seat and noticed that the seat I had been in the previous day was not occupied, I didn't think much about it at the time, so I proceeded to find my way forward and took the chair.

As expected Phillip Weidner began his opening statements, dressed in a black suit, with a long suit coat, something you might see on a hotel doorman, his pants tied with a rope, his long hair and black beard, almost made him appear to be sinister, certainly he had an unmistakable presence in the courtroom. As Weidner started his opening statements it was easy to see what his approach to the jury was going to be, his voice almost hypnotic, and his approach bordering on apoplectic. It was obvious that he was playing on the sympathy of the jury. He addressed the jury as "good and humble people" he even related his own humble beginnings in Illinois, saying he was a backwoods lawyer much like Abraham Lincoln. The con was on, no doubt his tactic was con-vincing the jury that not only was his client the underdog, but so was he. I looked around the room, the jury's reaction seemed mixed, and the spectators appeared mesmerized. I on the other had can recognize a con and this was it. He began by telling the jury that the state was rushing to judgment, he accused Mary Anne Henry of telling a terrible story, an artful illusion of terror, one of fear and deceit.

His main thrust was directed toward Larry's testimony. He stated the state was calling Larry an excellent witness. His rebuttal to this was calling Larry an "excellent example of drugs, and dreams, and desperation, and what the prosecutors can do with a man like this.

Weidner stressed the fact that the true nature of the crime was totally consistent with a "professional killing, a hit if you will". He stated that the killer set the boat on fire, calm and coolly in front of the whole town, drove back to town and disappeared. He went on to say that this is a mark of a professional killer. It was almost as though he was suggesting the murders were done by organized crime, in Craig Alaska? of all places.

His attack on Larry became personal; he brought up Larry drug use and abuse of alcohol. He made reference to Larry visiting a rehab center in Oregon. He was unrelenting in his barrage of despairing remarks. I started to take these accusations personally. There were times during his prancing about that I caught his eye, he knew I was not happy.

He went on to emphasis the possibility that Mark Coulthurst was dealing kilo's of cocaine, moving them aboard the Investor from the lower 48.

In his last statement he said "whoever did this, and it wasn't John Peel" because John Peel had no motive" whoever did this has vanished into thin air, vanished because of the States unwillingness to explore anyone else. "Everything the state will present will be circumstantial," nothing solid, no fingerprints, no real eye witnesses."

He then went on to blast the Police, stating there is missing evidence, "where is the gas can they found aboard the skiff? Where are the fingerprints that were supposed to be on the nozzle"? With this he thanked the jury and stated to Judge Schulz that his opening statements were complete.

It was now almost 11:30 and the judge dismissed the jury for lunch, telling the courtroom that the trial would resume at 1 p.m.

With the jury called back, it was now time for the actual trial to begin. Judge Schulz called the court to order at 1:35 p.m. much to everyone's surprise he said that the court would adjourn that it was decided that the jury would visit the boat dock in Craig. The media started scrambling out the door, families looked surprised. The judge ordered the bailiff to escort the jury members to an awaiting bus outside the back of the courthouse. The day was wet and windy, a chill to the bone type of day. I wasn't interested in going to the dock, so I went back to my room to wait for Larry, it was now about 2:30 and I knew that court was over for the day. This would give me time to get some rest and call home.

Once in my room I noticed that everything appeared to be in order, a quick once over failed to reveal anything out of the ordinary. Out of the corner of my eye I noticed the message light on my phone was blinking. My first thought was that my wife had called, leaving her with the business to run and it being her birthday, I thought it may be her. I called the front desk, they said the message read, I'm in room 106, and no name was left on the message. I immediately felt a sinking feeling, a feeling of concern, some fear. I was in room 103, Larry is in 104 this message came from room 106, too close for comfort. I thought about Larry, I hadn't seen him since the court let out; he had gone to the dock for the tour.

I slowly picked up the receiver and dialed 9 then the room number 106, the phone rang several times, my heart was racing, and the voice on the other end was to the point. "Boy come down here" no one called me boy, except my friend from Seattle, he was here, my fear subsided in an instant, I hung up the phone and immediately went to room 106. Opening the door was my friend, tall in stature, thin, and wearing his trademark sharkskin cowboy boots, we hugged and were both very glad to see each other. "What the hell have you gotten yourself into" he asked with a smile. "I'm not sure" I responded, as I told you on the phone something doesn't feel right, I know I'm being followed and I think it could be more than that. "Well my boy, I found these in your room". I looked in his hand and he held two small round discs. I immediately knew them to be "bugs" listening devices. I wasn't surprised, yet I was a little stunned. Here in Craig Alaska, here in the last frontier, who was listening and why. My friend then went on to say that one device was found inside the lamp near my bed, the other was found in Larry's room. I wanted to ask him how he had gotten in our rooms, but I didn't have to, I knew.

We sat down and tried to figure out, whom and why, the best we could come up with was the prosecution might want to know what Larry and I were talking about at night. The other could be the defense, I know they were puzzled as to whom I am and why I'm here I told my friend. His thoughts were a little more serious, he asks if I thought the murders were over drugs, I said I thought they were, having read Larry's massive book of testimony, I had thought that the drug angle was valid. I also told my friend that just seeing John Peel as much as I have, my judgment was he couldn't have acted alone; he just doesn't appear to have the balls. My friends reply was simple "I taught you to trust your gut, it has saved you more than once, and I trust your instincts". I asked him if he was going to stick around, his response was what I thought it would be, "no, I have to get home, you'll be fine". With that, we said our goodbyes, I know my friend too well, and he plays his cards close to the vest. I decided not to tell Larry.

Arriving at the courthouse on March 6th 1986, almost two years since the actual murders I found my seat, the same seat, I guess it was supposed to be my seat. Larry had gone into the area where the witnesses were to wait before being called to the stand. Everyone in the courtroom had suspected that Larry would be the first witness called by the prosecution. We were all surprised when the first witness called was the model maker, then the superintendent of the Columbia Ward Cove Cannery, who testified that he didn't sound the alarm on the day of the fire, which was in total contradiction of another witness testimony given to the Grand Jury. Even Larry Demmert Sr. preceded Larry to the stand, his testimony confirming that John Peel had never traveled to the scene of the fire.

Larry was an important witness for the state. Quite possibly the most important witness.

Larry's testimony was also important enough for Mary Anne Henry was willing to risk giving Larry immunity for his trial testimony. She later was to admit that giving Larry immunity scared her, because it gave Larry "an easy way out." He could have said that he was John Peel's skipper, and then just coped out by saying, "he's a nice guy, and that's all I can tell you."

Knowing Larry, I knew he would stand behind his testimony, he would step up.

As I saw Larry take the stand he looked scared, vulnerable, blinking nervously. His voice was hard to hear, he spoke in a very low tone, emotional from the start, and Larry didn't retreat into immunity. Assistant District Attorney Bob Blasco started out the questioning, Larry stood by his statement that he had seen a drunken John Peel climbing aboard the Investor on the night of the murders. He stood by his statement that he had seen John Peel on a North Cove dock with what looked like a rifle in his hand. He did say that he wasn't sure if the person that he thought he had seen in the wheelhouse of the Investor as it pulled away from the dock, was in fact John Peel. He had previously testified at the Grand Jury that it had been John Peel in the wheelhouse.

Larry's most difficult and emotional moment came when he was asked to describe how he felt when he was suddenly awakened the night of the murders. Larry paused, looked straight at me and for a brief moment I knew he was in trouble, I could see him holding back his emotions, his eyes filled with tears, he just starred at me. I smiled and nodded my head as if to say, go ahead, you can do this. "When I woke up I was real scared," he said. I have never been that scared in my life. I don't know why. It was like there was a danger in the air, and evil. It was just thick."

As Larry was testifying I noticed that John Peel had a blank expression on his face. His friend was testifying as to what he saw, incriminating him in a gruesome murder of eight people. Yet he showed no expression.

As Larry continued to testify, Mary Anne Henry now was asking the questions. Larry said he had found his H&R .22 caliber pistol in the wheelhouse of the Libby 8, he said this struck him odd because, "I usually keep it in my stateroom."

When asked if he had seen John Peel for those days surrounding the murders, Larry stated that John had not been around the boat much if any during the next two days, and at one point he had sent another crewman Brian Polinkus after him.

Larry said after about twenty minutes Brian hadn't returned so he himself went to find them. He went on to say that he had found them both at the Hill Bar. "I told them to get their asses down to the boat." John only stayed ten or fifteen minutes and he was gone Larry told Henry.

Larry went on to tell the jurors that the next time he had seen John Peel was the day the Investor was on fire. Larry said that he had been to the scene of the fire aboard his fathers boat the Cindy Sue and when they returned John Peel was standing on the cannery dock. "He appeared shook up, his face was red and he was breathing heavy." Larry asked Peel if he wanted to go out to the fire on the Cindy Sue. Larry said that John Peels response was "I don't want to go watch them burn." Larry said he found Peels response somewhat strange because no one knew for sure if anybody was on board the Investor. It was now 11:30 so Judge Schulz dismissed the jury for lunch and told everyone to return promptly at 1:30.

Larry left the stand and walked past me, as he did, he bent down to tell me to meet him outside, and we would grab a bite together. As I had done every time the court was dismissed, I waited for John Peel and his attorneys to pass me before I would leave. This time my eyes were not fixed on John Peel but directly at Phillip Weidner. I just smiled and followed him and John Peel and Weidner's investigator out the double doors into the hallway. I walked past them as they stopped to speak to Peels family. I could feel the stares burning a hole in my back as I walked away. I thought to myself. Fuck you, I've got you and you know it.

Larry was waiting outside the courthouse, having a well deserved smoke. As I approached he let out a big grin, as if he was happy that ordeal was over. He asked me how he was doing and I told him he was great, but assured him that this was just the beginning. The day was unusual, the sun was actually shining, a rare event in March, in Ketchikan Alaska.

Larry suggested we walk a little bit, so we headed down the street, the only place that served a quick lunch was a bar. As we entered the first thing I noticed was the dust and smoke covered windows, the old floors that creaked when we walked on them, this bar could tell stories. We found a corner table and sat down. Just as we had gotten seated the waitress-bartender came up and told us the daily specials, chicken sandwich with chips, or a French dip sandwich with fries. Both Larry and I ordered the French dip.

Our chairs faced the door, as it opened we saw Mary Anne Henry and Bob Blasco enter. Larry said "are they following me?" I assured him that even prosecutors need to eat. They approached our table and Larry stood to greet them, He introduced me to both of them as a friend from Oregon. They were polite saying that they were glad that Larry had support while he was here. We exchanged pleasantries and they found a table near the bar. Larry tried to talk of things other than his testimony, family, weather, girlfriend, and fishing. I knew he wanted me to comment on how his testimony was going. I let him ramble, knowing this was just a diversion for his mind. When he took a breath I asked him how he was holding up. He said that I think I'm doing ok, I stated that I thought he was doing fine, but told him that when the defense had their shot, all gloves were going to be off. He just nodded his head; I knew he was going to be drilled like an old well. In the back of my mind I knew it was going to get ugly. My hope was that the prosecutors were going to step up and protect him.

It wasn't going to be long until this scenario became reality. When we were finished, we took a long walk down to the boat dock, we just meandered looking at the various boats that were moored. Every once in awhile Larry would speak, pointing to a particular boat, he would tell me all about the vessel, how it worked, where it had been, who owned it, and anything else that he thought I needed to know. It was now getting close to the afternoon session so we headed toward the courthouse. I could sense Larry getting nervous, so I tried to make light of the situation, but knowing full well it was falling on deaf ears.

The bailiff called the court to order, and Judge Schulz asked if the prosecutor was ready to continue. Assistant District Attorney Bob Blasco now was doing the questioning. I thought this strange because it seemed like Mary Anne Henry had gained Larry's trust and he was speaking freely with her. After Blasco started his questioning I saw their tactic. Blasco started his questioning by asking Larry why he started using valium. Larry paused for a second and responded that he got a prescription for the muscle relaxer when the troopers started asking him questions about his friend John Peel in March of 1984. Larry went on to say that he started increasing his usage because of "stress, fear, and emotion" associated with the thought that his friend had killed the Investor crew, especially the little children. "I didn't want to testify against my friend," he said. Larry went on to say that he was "so afraid that I purchased a gun, for protection".

Blasco then asked Larry why he had withheld information from the state troopers. Larry replied "I didn't want to be involved in this case" and besides John Peel was a longtime friend. "I grew up with the attitude you don't talk to cops, you don't rat out a friend."

Larry went on to explain why he had downplayed his testimony before both grand juries, "I was hoping to make myself less valuable. "I was trying to soften up my testimony" he told Blasco.

I could see where this was headed; Blasco was trying to get these questions answered before the defense could get at Larry. I had a sense that this was about to get real ugly. Blasco asked Larry if he was satisfied with his testimony. Larry responded "I only changed my testimony as much as I needed to make the truth known". With that Blasco stated he was finished with Larry.

Judge Schulz asked the defense, if they were ready to cross-examine? Not surprising, Phillip Weidner asked that for a recess for the day, he asked that his cross examination be put off until the morning. I knew this was a stall tactic, not that Weidner wasn't ready, in fact you could tell he was chomping at the bit to get to Larry, this was being done so that Larry would have time to stew, to maybe forget what he had just said to Bob Blasco. I had no doubt that tomorrow would be brutal. Judge Schulz agreed to dismiss the trial for the day, saying that court would resume promptly at 9:30.

The prosecution knew Phillip Weidner was going after Larry. They just weren't sure where he would start. They seemed to be a vast amount of choices and the state's careful handling of Larry tried to anticipate them all. Weidner would no doubt study Larry's testimony and pick it apart, looking for any opportunity to attack.

Larry met me at the motel around 4:30 we had some dinner. I asked Larry if he wanted to go over the testimony together, maybe he would feel better prepared. His response surprised me. "No, I'm ok" he said. With that we parted and went our separate ways. I returned to my room and called home. Talking to my wife, I realized how much I missed my life. I had gotten wrapped up in this case and it seemed as if I couldn't shake it. I kept seeing the pictures of the burning boat, hearing the reports of the bodies seeping through the charred ruins. The pictures of the two little children, so young, so innocent, gone forever. No trace of the small boy, just ashes. I couldn't let it go. I told my wife I would come home if she needed me. She reassured me that I was doing the right thing, and I should stay. I guess I was just feeling lonely. I couldn't imagine what Larry was feeling.

My wake up call came too soon. It was 7a.m. pitch black out and pouring rain, not a good day for what would lie ahead.

Larry and I met at our usual time, and had a good breakfast; we talked about everything except the day ahead. I told Larry that I had a good talk with my wife and she wished him well. He thanked me for her well wishes. A long silence followed, then Larry said he had asked his girlfriend to come to Ketchikan, looking for a reaction from me, I said I thought it was a good idea, remembering my feeling last night.

We took a taxi to the courthouse, it was pouring rain and the distance from the street to the doors of the courthouse provided ample time to get soaked. The court was called to order, and as expected Larry was called to the stand.

"Good morning, Mr. Demmert," Phillip Weidner said as he stood and faced Larry for the first time.

"Good morning" Larry replied. Then Weidner went for the jugular.

"Mr. Demmert," Weidner continued, "you are a drug addict, are you not?" With this Bob Blasco shot out of his chair. "I object, Your Honor," he said, his voice full of rage at Weidner's statement.

"It's relevant, Your Honor," Weidner shot back.

Blasco responded, "There's no foundation for this Your Honor."

"I'll sustain this objection," Schulz replied.

It was easy to see where this was headed, Larry just sat there, appearing calm on the outside, but I knew he was churning on the inside.

Weidner continued, asking Larry the same question in several different ways, Blasco objected every time, and his objections were sustained each and every time. The questioning and objections had gone on for over fifteen minutes; still Larry hadn't been able to respond.

Judge Schulz ruled that "only Mr. Demmerts drug use during the times that he gave testimony will be relevant." Weidner kept after Larry, often skirting dangerously close to the limits set by the judge. Blasco kept a close vigilance on Weidner, holding his tongue until Weidner was close to asking a question that would require an objection. Blasco and Mary Anne Henry knew that a question even one that would sustain an objection would be heard by the jury. Having been on several jury's I know that a question once asked has an impact, even if the objection is sustained, even if the judge tells the jury to disregard the question, the damage is done.

I can see Weidner is a pro at this tactic. Weidner again asked Larry in a general way "there was some general talk about whether or not you had used drugs." The judge was not amused.

Weidner quickly changed the direction of his questioning. He attacked Larry for his multiple meeting with the prosecutors, suggesting they were "telling you what they expected your testimony should be."

Before the day was over, Weidner also attacked Larry for his identification of John Peel, saying that Larry had changed his testimony regarding the color of the shirt John Peel was wearing. "Since you were trying to convince someone you had seen John Peel, you thought you'd throw in the flannel shirt, isn't that true?" Larry denied Weidners accusation.

Larry denied Weidners accusation. Weidner just wouldn't let up. I could see that Larry was getting upset, I really couldn't blame him. I would have blown up long before now.

After facing Weidners barrage for a half a day, the defense attorney finally relented. Larry was able to step down from the stand at least for the day. Larry hadn't buckled under Weidners cross examination. The prosecution was able to be optimistic. Larry had known John Peel for nearly twenty years. He had spent the entire summer working next to Peel. Under Weidner's questioning, he had revealed that he was standing "twenty or thirty feet" away from John Peel when he saw him struggling over the rail of the Investor. I think even Weidner knew that this testimony was damaging.

Larry and I met up at the motel, I had arranged a surprise for him, I had flown his girlfriend in from Bellingham and she was waiting in his room. I told Larry I would meet him for dinner around 6:30 and we parted ways. I wasn't in my room five minutes and the phone rang, it was Larry thanking me. I could tell in his voice that his surprise had lightened his day. I told Larry that maybe he would want to skip dinner and order room service, he laughed and agreed. I told him I was going to walk downtown and grab a bite later; I'd see him in the morning. I told him to get some sleep; again he laughed and hung up.

For the next five days, Phillip Weidner lashed out at Larry mercilessly. One comfort Larry had was that he had his own attorney in the courtroom to cover his ass. Even with that, Weidner attacked Larry on the drug addiction and police intimidation parts of his testimony. He directed his attack on Larry's drug usage, even though the judge had warned him repeatedly, Weidner didn't let up. There were times I just wanted to jump up and defend Larry myself. This line of questioning went on relentlessly, objections from Larry's attorney, objections from the district attorney, reprimands from the judge, still Weidner continued. The judge finally had enough, he dismissed the jury and told Weidner to get out his checkbook, he was going to fine him every time he approached the drug usage or police intimidation.

Judge Schulz went even further to make sure that Weidner didn't continue his rant. He asked an Alaska State Trooper to come to the courtroom. If Weidner disobeyed his orders this time, Schulz was going to send him to jail. Weidner knew it was Friday and he wouldn't get a judge to let him out of jail until Monday. The trooper that showed up was Sergeant John Glass. He came in full uniform, and was ready to take Weidner away. I could tell that Phillip Weidner for the first time since the trial had begun had met his match. Upon seeing Sergeant Glass, Weidner asked to approach the bench. "There's a state trooper back there in uniform," Weidner protested.

The judge said "I know, I called him."

"Well I feel intimidated," Weidner said.

"Good," the judge shot back, "That's exactly how I want you to feel."

Weidner was on his best behavior for the rest of the day. Sergeant Glass was obviously irritated with Weidner and there was no doubt that he was looking forward to hauling Weidner off to jail. I was later to find out that Sergeant Glass had more than a professional interest in how Phillip Weidner was treating the defense. It was now March 20th Larry had been on the stand for five straight days.

Weidner finally rested his case; Judge Schulz asked Mary Anne Henry if they had any further questions for Mr. Demmert, Henry replied that she had no further questions. With that Larry's ordeal was over.

Mary Anne Henry stated that she had found Larry Demmert a creditable witness, "concerned with telling the truth." This was done in an interview with the media.

Larry and his girlfriend met me for dinner. We discussed his testimony. He asked me if I thought he had done a good job. If I thought the jury had believed him. I told him I thought he had done a great job, and I was sure the jury had seen his honesty.

We talked a lot about what he was going to do now that his testimony was over, their plans for getting married and just small talk. I told Larry I had a flight out in the morning and I had to pack. Both he and his girlfriend thanked me for being there; I could see that Larry truly meant it. I left both of them in the restaurant and walked back to the motel, as I walked I knew in my gut that John Peel had been involved but I didn't feel they would get him, I just felt something was not right.

My flight didn't leave until 9:30 the next morning; it would arrive in Seattle at 11:40. My wife had made plans to meet me there and we would fly home to Seaside in our own plane. I was tired and looking forward to going home. I had one last thing to do before I could leave Ketchikan; I had to get rid of the listening devices my friend had found in our rooms. My first thought was to give one to Phillip Weidner and the other to Mary Anne Henry. I had second thoughts, I knew Weidner would deny it and run to the Judge for a mistrial. Mary Anne Henry would immediately blame Weidner and the trial would be held up for an indefinite time so I decided to send them anonymously to Judge Schulz. I would let him decide what to do. I put them in an envelope and addressed them to the Honorable Judge Schulz. I would drop them off on my way out of town.

⌐

After eight months and more than two million dollars, closing arguments in Alaska's longest criminal trial were to begin. Both sides filed motions requesting Judge Schulz prohibit parts of almost all testimony, both for the defense and prosecution. Mary Anne Henry asked Judge Schulz to prohibit Weidner from referring to almost 40 topics during closing arguments. One of the most vital areas of her concern was Peel's attorney referring to drug dealing by Mark Coulthurst. Judge Schulz banned drug references and six other topics, the closing arguments were going to begin.

A surprising move by the prosecution found Pat Gullufsen giving the closing argument for the State. Mary Anne Henry had stepped aside. Gullufsen had a huge task in front of him; he had to summarize eight months of testimony, often heated and try not to put the jury asleep.

Gullufsen made light of the defense, saying that Weidner's assertion that the murders were carried out by professionals. The theory that the murders were done by someone other than John Peel. Weidner never was actually allowed to introduce the drug assassin's evidence.

Gullufsen reminded the jury of all the testimony that had been given that pointed to John Peel. He went down the list of witnesses, one by one, reciting the actual points of interest in each testimony. The jury was riveted to Gullufsen, watching every move he made, listening carefully to every word. Weidner called Gullufsen's remarks to the jury "speculation and conjecture" Weidner's co-counsel called Gullufsen "boring and tedious".

Phillip Weidner was not about to be undone by Pat Gullufson. When Weidner took his place in front of the jury he cautioned the jury not to be swept away "by fear", not to judge by speculation and conjecture. Weidner then went on to discredit all of the testimony, picking apart everyone who had testified for the state. Focusing on Larry, he asked, "Would you rely on Larry Demmert if your life was at stake?"

Weidner got chastised by Judge Schulz when he started addressing the jurors by name. He told Weidner that addressing the jury by name was improper and told him not to do it again. The next day found Weidner and Brant McGee attacking every witness, all the missing evidence, they attacked the sloppy police work, the inept investigators, and the lack of follow-up on prospective leads.

After Weidner had attacked every witness, dismissed all of the evidence, he was now finished with his closing statement. The customary procedure in any trial by jury, allows the state the last word. Pat Gullufsen took this opportunity to address John Peel's alibis, which he said "were flimsy at best". Gullufsen then turned his wrath directly to John Peel, facing Peel he read the names of the murdered victims, one by one, in a slow baritone voice he listed them. Starting with the two small children, then to their parents, then each crewmember. He asked the jury to "keep looking at Mr. Peel, because the evidence puts their blood on his hands".

With those remarks Pat Gullufsen and the State of Alaska closed the book on the Investor murder case. It was soon to be in the hands of the jury.

The jury was sequestered at the Super 8 motel one day before the closing arguments had ended. The actual deliberations began Saturday, August 23rd 1986. There were only twelve jurors left, the minimum required for a complete jury. This put the state in a very precarious position, if one of the remaining jurors could not continue the case would automatically end in a mistrial.

The verdict could go several ways for John Peel. If the jury found him guilty of all eight murders and arson he faced 800 years in prison. If they found him not guilty beyond a reasonable doubt they would have to set him free. Judge Schulz had decided that Peel could not found guilty of lesser charges. Over the next several days the jury requested several item of evidence including transcripts from several witnesses.

On the sixth day of deliberations, the jury returned to the courthouse earlier than usual it was 8:30 a.m. earlier than Judge Schulz had recommended. At 2:10 p.m. the jury sent a note to Judge Schulz. The note said they were "unable to reach a unanimous verdict." The judge called in the attorneys from both sides. People in the courtroom sensed something was about to happen, they just didn't know what it was. Judge Schulz asked the jury foreman "how long has it been since there has been any movement." The jury foreman paused and replied "I would say the last was this afternoon." The foreman then stated "they can go no further".

Judge Schulz looked concerned, his expression was serious. Finally he declared to the jurors, "I'm going to discharge you. Words can't express my thanks," With that the jury was cautioned not to talk with anyone about their conclusions and keep silent about what went on in the jury room. They were dismissed at 3:45. With the jury gone Judge Schulz declared a mistrial. A second trial was scheduled to begin January 20, 1987.

The State Attorney General Hal Brown had been in contact with Judge Schulz after the mistrial, he asked Schulz what he thought about a retrying John Peel. Judge Schulz was quick to respond. "It doesn't matter what I think," Schulz told him. "This case has to be retried. You have to have a verdict one way or the other. You just can't walk away from an eight count murder case." They both agreed that the case would probably be moved, it would also stretch the budget. The first trial cost almost $2 million.

Before Attorney general Brown made a decision he called in the jury foreman from the first trial. "I just want to chat with the foreman to learn how the jury was split on the nine counts, he stated." He also sent his director of criminal prosecution to Washington State to interview Larry Demmert. The case had turned on Larry's credibility which the defense had attacked relentlessly. The criminal prosecutor met with Larry and determined that he in fact was a creditable witness and a trustworthy person.

On October 10th, 1986, Alaska Attorney General Hal Brown announced his decision. The State of Alaska would retry John Peel, his statement read "The Investor case was the most notorious case in southeast Alaska history. A jury should decide."

Phillip Weidner had always opposed holding the trial in Ketchikan. He filed many motions, one asking to postpone the trial from January to December, 1987 another was to let John Peel get a job and move out of his parents home. Judge Schulz was waiting for Weidner to request a change of venue, that motion wasn't forthcoming. Schulz was surprised.

It was November 28th; Judge Schulz was scheduled to hear the defense motions. District Attorney Mary Anne Henry surprised him, she was about to blow this case sky high. Judge Schulz asked her if she was ready to respond to the defense arguments, she said "Your Honor," her tone was serious, "I'm not prepared to discuss that at this time, except for whether I will be filing one motion based on a matter that was brought to my attention three days ago, and I also would like to briefly set forth the state's position in that matter at this time."

"Go ahead," Schulz responded, totally unaware of what was about to take place. Mary Anne Henry dropped the bomb. "The matter that was brought to my attention three days ago requires the state as part of its ethical responsibility to pursue, both factually and legally. Let it be known that I cannot participate ethically in this proceeding any longer until these matters are resolved. If a motion needs to filed on those matters, I will file it in two weeks.

"You are talking about the matter that was brought to your attention three days ago?" Schulz asked.

"Yes," Henry replied'

Before she left the courtroom she said the issue was extremely serious. Serious enough that neither Judge Schulz nor Phillip Weidner might be able to participate in John Peel's second trial. Both Weidner and Schulz appeared stunned.

The mystery issue, Schulz was soon to find out, was that Phillip Weidner had been romantically liked with Judge Schulz law clerk or, more accurately, his former law clerk. The word was that they were lovers. To make matters worse she had only recently left her position as Schulz's clerk. Even worse, she took a job on September 1, 1986 with the Ketchikan Public Defender's office, the same office that represented John Peel. Mary Anne Henry demanded that Judge Schulz remove himself from the Peel case. If he refused to step down she wanted him disqualified. The romance between Schulz's law clerk and Phillip Weidman was in her mind unethical. Henry was convinced that Weidner had an unfair advantage. The law clerk had no doubt delivered Weidner every thought and attitude that Judge Schulz had during the first trial. An unfair advantage, Henry stated.

To make matters even worse it seems the law clerk had dated one of the investigators when they lived in Petersburg, and a second defense investigator had dated the best friend of the law clerk. Henry detailed a host of other of other charges against the law clerk, which Henry insisted made it impossible for Judge Schulz to continue with the Investor murder case. Henry stated that Judge Schulz had ordered the bank to produce John Peel's bank record, and told the bank not to discuss those records with the prosecution. Henry also raised questions about Schulz's failure to inform the State of the law clerks relationship with Weidner, especially since the law clerk was a "potential witness."

Judge Schulz and Phillip Weidner both went on the defensive, in a turn about Weidner even defended Schluz, saying that he presided over the Peel trial with complete professionalism. Weidner also criticized Mary Anne Henry for suggesting that Schulz excuse himself for the "appearance of impropriety," while serving as lead prosecutor in cases where she had a "close personal relationship" with police officers involved.

Weidner went on to say "this includes the case we are now involved in. Officer Glass was called as a material witness for the State and actually examined by Ms. Henry. I ask whether Ms. Henry will excuse herself from further participation in this case due to her past relationship with Officer Glass."

In the next few days Mary Anne Henry managed to raise Judge Schulz's temper on more than one occasion. If Schulz agreed to change venue and remove himself from the case, the state would agree to drop its complaints against him. Judge Schulz refused to take the deal. "That's blackmail" he said.

The final decision did not rest with Judge Schulz, under Alaska law; the disqualification request went before another judge. On February 11, 1987, a full two months after the controversy broke; Judge Victor D. Carlson handed down his decision. He noted the facts in the case were not disputed. Judge Schulz's law clerk had declared her romantic involvement with Phillip Weidner "soon after the mistrial was declared." It was also noted that the involvement "has apparently continued." Judge Carlson also found it reasonable to assume that the law clerk had learned the "innermost thoughts of the Judge" concerning the case and its participants. "The law clerk possesses this fund of information and it is impossible to expect that none of it will be shared with the people with whom she is involved, and the greater the degree of involvement, the greater the degree of sharing."

Judge Carlson then ruled "It is ordered that the Honorable Thomas R. Schulz is disqualified for cause." The only saving grace afforded to Judge Schulz was that he was allowed to pick his successor.

HOME AGAIN

It had been just three weeks since I left home to support Larry. It seemed like forever. It was good to see my wife, my patients, and just get back into a routine. Larry called me about once a week, keeping me updated regarding the trial. His calls became further apart as the weeks progressed, eventually stopping altogether. I became wrapped up in daily living and the trial became less and less important to me.

Somewhere in the back of my mind I knew that the outcome wouldn't be what the families wanted it to be. John Peel was guilty for some part of the crime, but I felt that the prosecution wasn't going to be able to prove beyond a reasonable doubt that he had committed these heinous murders.

In the months to come my life continued on a normal pace, treatment continued, lives changed and daily drama became the norm.

Larry called me sometime around November of 1986 saying the trial had ended in a mistrial. He didn't know much of the details he just said that the trial had stopped. I wasn't surprised. I would find out later that there was a "mystery issue" that no one could have foreseen. Just another strange twist in what was to be a continuous miscarriage of justice.

I later found out that there was to be a new trial. The second trial was going to be held in Juneau, Alaska. The Juneau Superior Court was to be the site of the new trial which was scheduled to begin sometime in January of 1988.

I spoke to Larry and informed him that I wouldn't be able to attend this trial.

As January 1988 approached I couldn't help but think of Larry and the forthcoming trial. I could still see the photos of the charred remains of the people burned aboard the Investor, the pictures of the two small children in happier times, gone forever. These haunted me almost daily.

My wife's battle with cancer was just beginning; it was to become all consuming, taking every waking moment of my attention. In 1992 we sold our business and retired. Still living on the Oregon coast we settled into a life that was slower paced and much less stressful. Taking care of my wife was my primary concern, her cancer had gone into remission and I was left with nothing much to do. One day while we were walking on the beach my wife turned to me out of the blue and asked "what ever happened to that trial in Alaska, did they convict that guy?" I answered her by saying" I don't know" she went on to ask me if I ever thought about the trial. She being a trained therapist, could sense my discomfort, we had had discussions in the past about my feelings when it came to the little children that were murdered. She knew that I wanted to follow up with this, she knew I needed too.

At her insistence I began to make plans to research the outcome of the Investor murders. She insisted I go to Alaska to see what I could find out.

This is where my investigation begins, what I found out would change my life forever.

Bad People Do Bad Things
January 1986

The day was nothing out of the ordinary, I arrived at the center about 8:30, and the patients had been eating breakfast. I walked through the dinning room and acknowledged them; they were cleaning up and getting ready for the first scheduled event that began at 9: am sharp. Schedules were important in a treatment setting. Structure and responsibility is something that we stress. Most of the patients had long ago given up responsibilities and defiantly were un-structured.

As I approached my office I had to pass the admitting area, I looked in to see who may be there if anyone, not surprising I observed two people one female about 25, blonde and rather tall maybe 5'10. She had a professional appearance and I could tell she was not the one being admitted. Next to her sat a man in his late twenties, short light brown hair, stocky build, I figured him to be 5'9 maybe a little taller, it was hard top tell he was bent over in the chair.

I continued on to my office, after unlocking the door and putting my coat away, I switched on my desk lamp. It was mid winter and the days were dark and dreary. My office had been re-decorated by my wife several times, however this time she had actually listened to my input. My desk faced the pacific ocean which was only a stones throw from my window, a soft leather couch and matching chair were situated so as to capture the view for anyone sitting there, a small round table made of burl wood held a sailboat figurine and a brass floor lamp was placed in a position to brighten the sitting area. All in all it was the quiet place I had finally earned. Having been in the treatment business for a long time, I was getting tired, I had begun taking more time off and caring a light case load. Looking at my messages that had piled up over night, my eyes were drawn to one in particular. A Man called from Anchorage, wants to come to treatment A.S.A.P. money not a problem. I scanned the rest of the messages, and kept coming back to this one. I picked up the phone and called the admitting area, I asked if they had taken the message and the response was "he's here". I remembered the man in the admitting area as I had come in, I thought to myself, he got here quick, anytime I tried to get a flight somewhere it was never that quick.

Just then there was a figure standing in my doorway, because I kept the lights dimmed I couldn't make out a face, I asked if I could be of some help?, a voice replied "I just brought my boyfriend into treatment from Alaska, I was told to come and see you about arrangements" As my eyes adjusted, I could see it was the young lady that I had seen with the man in admitting. I asked her to come in and sit down. I inquired if she would like anything, tea, coffee; she said no thank you they had eaten on the flight in. I told her of my amazement at the speed in which they had arrived, I looked at my message the time read 10:30 pm. She smiled and said she worked for the airline and was able to pull some strings and get a flight out, the last one, she said they had arrived in Portland and rented a car and were here about 2 a.m. She then said they had found a room just down the beach.

I asked her some questions, got some releases signed and was about to direct her to the business office when she leaned forward and said to me" this needs to be discreet he doesn't want to use his real name." She then handed me an envelope, upon opening it I realized it was full payment for treatment, payment in $100.00 bills. Payment in cash was nothing out of the ordinary; however the request for discretion maybe, not the request itself but just the way she looked when making it that appeared strange. She appeared frightened, I assured her that we would honor the request, and do everything we could to help her significant other. I had yet to learn his name, she hadn't said, I didn't ask.

After a brief explanation of what was expected of her and what she could expect from us, she rose from the chair and walked out of my office. I had no idea that our lives would be forever changed as a result of this meeting.

The day proceded as usual, nothing unexpected, just treatment as usual. The young man was placed in de-tox for observation and treatment went on as scheduled.

It was about the fifth day after admitting Mark that I was to have any real contact with him. From all outside appearances he seemed like a regular guy, he said he was a construction worker, had lived in Alaska most of his life and had "got tied up with the wrong crowd". He went on to explain that his cocaine addiction was slow coming but had taken its toll. He was unable to find work because he just wasn't reliable, his girlfriend had a young son and he was afraid that it was becoming dangerous for him. This wasn't a unique pattern for a cocaine addict; I had heard this story a thousand times, only the names change.

My years of experience told me that Mark was only telling me what I wanted to hear, a fine story, yet there was the fact that he had paid cash and insisted that no records be kept. Something wasn't ringing true, yet I let Mark tell his story. As the days went by I could see that Mark really wanted to get clean, he tried hard and didn't balk at anything I asked of him. He participated in all group functions, was never late, and always helped anyone who was having trouble. We actually started to become good friends. I shared with him my trip to Alaska to support a former patient who had testified in a murder trial in Ketchikan, he was attentive yet seemed nervous, he tried to change the subject. I told him of the incident, he said he had read about it, and thought the guy got off. I said that he however I still thought he was guilty. Mark replied "well that's the legal system it's not always fair, money talks". I found the statement somewhat strange, but knew he was right. The conversation went in a different direction after that and nothing more was said about the incident.

Time came and it was close to Marks release so I scheduled a conference with his girlfriend. I had scheduled it for a Saturday which was also our family day. Mark and his girlfriend participated during the day and many areas of their relationship were addressed as well as what Mark was going to do for work, where he would live and just the regular chatter. All the while I could sense that Mark wasn't paying a lot of attention to anything that was being discussed. Mark didn't seem to be worried about finances; actually he didn't seem to be worried about anything. The couple seemed happy, but I could sense they were withholding something, a secret, an area that was not going to be addressed, not going to be discussed. I knew the secret, and he knew that I knew it. We shook hands and said our goodbyes.

Mark was discharged and before he left he invited me to come visit them in Alaska, I received invitations all the time, but always wanting to see Alaska again, I said I might just take him up on his invite. With that we parted, I didn't see Mark or his girlfriend again until later in the year, when I received that frantic phone call from Alaska.

It was January of 1987, my wife and I had finally decided to retire and do some traveling. We decided that we wanted to see Taipei. We had some friends who lived in Taiwan and they had invited us over to visit. We decided that we would incorporate a stop in Hong Kong China on our way home. The trip was scheduled for late December. As December approached we made arrangements for the house to be looked after and the mail to be collected, we would be gone about three weeks.

The flight to Taiwan was over 18 hours; the flight took polar route, over the North Pole, which I later found somewhat ironic. We were told to stay awake on the flight because when we arrived in Taipei it would be late and then we could sleep.

The culture shock was immediate; we hailed a cab which was our first mistake. The cabs in Taipei number in the thousands, and it seemed that they were all on the streets at once. If it wasn't the cab traffic it was the bicycle traffic. The cab ride was horrific; it seems that they can use the sidewalks if it serves the purpose. So all I really could see were bicycles scattering and the sounds of horns honking. We had made reservations at the Grand Palace Hotel. The hotel is an iconic Taipei Landmark; it was constructed at the whim of Madame Chang Kai Check, the wife of China's ruler. It was constructed by over a thousand Chinese workers and was completed in the late 1960's or early 70's. The Hotel is constructed to resemble a multistoried Chinese Palace. The interior is a red painted gold leaf chasm, huge tall ceilings, ornate Chinese décor, everything seemed larger than life.

It was late and we had taken our friends advice and had stayed awake during the long flight. We checked in and went right to bed. The next morning found us somewhat tired from the jet lag. I called our friends and agreed to meet them for dinner later that evening. We dressed and decided to take in the sights. We did all the tourist stuff and got lost several times, but all in all had a good day. We arrived back in our Hotel around 3p.m. and took a nap. Our friends arrived about 5:30 and we headed to a real Taiwanese dinner. The restaurant was crowded with locals; they were well dressed and appeared to be enjoying themselves. Our friends had called ahead and reserved a large table overlooking the city. The food never stopped coming, I could tell that this experience was going to be just that, an experience. The first item to arrive was the fish head soup. I had a hard time getting by the beady eyes looking at me from the large bowl in the center of the table. Next came a dish I could not recognize, afraid to ask I just sampled a taste. My wife was having a great time, although the real ivory chop sticks were giving her some trouble. The next dish pushed me over the top, it was a squid dish and the squid was still alive, I had to pass on this one, then a pork dish arrived with the head of the pig placed at the end of the platter. This was going from bad to worse. I could not insult my friends and refuse, so I just picked around my plate. At one point I excused myself and went outside, I had to get some air. Outside and two doors down my eyes caught sight of a Burger King, yes a Burger King, and yes I got a hamburger and wolfed it down. Returning to my wife and friends I could honestly say I wasn't feeling very well and I excused myself from any further torment at the dining table. We talked about everything and nothing, their children were both in collage at the University of California, and they were coming to the states soon to visit them. My wife and I extended them an invitation to visit us in Oregon and they said they would. We parted ways that evening and took another death defying act in a taxi to our Hotel.

We had plans to take an afternoon flight to Hong Kong the next day.

Getting to the airport took over two hours, just 20 miles in two hours. Customs was not much better, but we finally boarded our flight to Hong Kong. I had made reservations at the Holiday Inn in Kowloon. The hotel had a great view of Victoria Harbor. It was midday when we arrived and the weather allowed us to walk around the area and take in the sights. Our room was elegant and vey comfortable. It was my wife's birthday and I had ordered a beautiful flower arrangement in advance, it was waiting for her when we arrived.

We had decided to take the air-boat over to the Island of Macau the next day. It was the closest we could get to mainland China. We spent the evening in the hotel and had a wonderful dinner in the restaurant atop the hotel. The view allowed us to see the beautiful harbor at night. When we awoke in the morning and opened our blinds we could see the boat traffic in the harbor. It came in all sizes, freighters delivering everything from autos to Budweiser beer. Small watercraft darting in and out of the harbor, we caught our first glimpse of Chinese Junks, the boats that I had only previously seen in books or movies. They were in all shapes and sizes, some were motor powered, and others had small sails. We also noticed what appeared to be a small floating market. After coffee we went for a walk down to the harbor. I wanted to get a closer look at the flotilla that made up this market place. As we crossed the courtyard outside the hotel we noticed several older people doing Tai Chi, their slow motion was an art in itself. I had studied Tai Chi for many years and even I was intrigued with the elderly and their daily routine. Their motions were all in sync and their steadiness and focus was a thing of beauty. I just stood there mesmerized. Just watching brought calm over me.

We continued on our walk and came upon the floating market. It was dozens of small flat bottomed boats all pushed together and selling their goods. Everything from fish to vegetables, from clothing to house wares. Entire families were on these small boats, small children hanging on to their mothers, young boys making sure the boats kept close to shore. From an outsiders view it looked like chaos, but with closer examination is was a well choreographed daily occurrence.

We wondered around for some time, going from shop to shop, experiencing the local flavor. I looked at some suits, suits in an hour. I passed on these. My wife bought some gifts for friends. And we found her a beautiful pearl necklace for her birthday.

We caught the afternoon air-boat to Macau. I had never been aboard an air-boat before; we slowly taxied out from the dock and turned toward Macau. As the boat picked up speed the noise was deafening.

The boat lifted off and skimmed the top of the water at forty miles an hour. It would take an hour and a half to reach Macau. Stepping from the boat I could sense a dark secretive city. The streets were crowded and very noisy. We walked up the narrow streets. The smells were almost too much to take. There were areas where the sewer flowed into the ditches. We walked to a point in the town where we could see Mainland China. It was divided off by a ten foot high barbed wire fence. There was a small viewing area that allowed us to take pictures beneath a sign that said China. We did the usual picture taking and walked back to the main part of Macau. We had some lunch and my wife wanted to go to a gambling parlor. This was long before any real Casinos were planned for Macau. Their "casinos" were small, crowded, smelly and dimly lit. They had hundreds of machines, Pa Chinco machines were everywhere. My wife had managed to find a blackjack table. She was the only woman at the table, she was a very good blackjack player and she had amassed a crowd around her. Edging my way through the crowd I noticed she had a large stack of chips in front of her. The dealer seemed nervous and was looking around for some direction. I could see him looking to his left. Standing there was a huge Chinese man with a well tailored suit, he just nodded and the game proceeded. My wife won a huge bet, I leaned over to her a said we might want to cash out. Our boat left in a few minutes and I really didn't want to get stuck here. With that she got up from the table, to my surprise the crowd started clapping and bowing, I was later to learn that this was an expression of approval. I noticed the large man that was standing nearby, starting to head toward us. I really didn't know what to expect. He bowed to my wife and spoke in a polite manner. He offered to escort us to the cashier, once there my wife cashed in over two thousand dollars. He then offered to have a car take us to the ferry terminal. I wasn't sure if this was a good thing or not. We agreed to his offer and he walked us outside and put us in the limousine.

Once we got to the ferry terminal we had to clear Chinese security. The security saw our arrival in the Limo and waved us right through.

We had had an exciting day, and could hardly wait to get back to the Hotel and get some rest. The boat arrived after midnight and we walked back to our room. It wasn't hard to fall asleep, we were exhausted.

It was about 9a.m. when we were awakened by the phone. I was half asleep when I heard the voice on the other end, it was Marks girlfriend, and she was hysterical, sobbing, saying that Mark had just been arrested. She was panicked; the police had kicked in her door in the early morning hours and awakened her and her son. They had ransacked her house and taken her into custody and later released her. Her seven year old son had been allowed to go to babysitters. I told her to take a breath, calm down; I was struggling to make sense of this whole thing. I asked her what Mark had done. She said all she knew was he was arrested in a Mall parking lot, by Alaska Fish and Game. They had found polar bear skins and walrus tusks, cash and what appeared to be several pounds of cocaine in his car. They had found more cocaine in the house. She swore she didn't know it was there. I needed to get some coffee, so I handed my wife the phone while I went to wash my face and order room service. Upon returning from the bathroom I noticed my wife had hung up the phone, I was somewhat surprised, and my wife said that she would call back in a few hours after she had picked up her son and had learned more about Mark.

The coffee came and I had a chance to clear my head. I had to think, this wasn't like Mark. I knew his focus on detail, I knew he was very good at what he did, something wasn't right, he would never have any product in his house, and he would never put his girlfriend or her son in this situation.

My wife and I discussed several scenarios, all coming to the same conclusion, that Mark had been under surveillance, he didn't know it and he fucked up.

We decided to not sit and wait for the return call. We had only one more day in Hong Kong and wanted to see as much of the city as we could. We took the cable car to the top of the hillside overlooking the city. The view was breathtaking and it was easy to see why so many people loved Hong Kong, it was so alive and so vibrant. Houses stacked upon houses, apartment buildings appeared to touch the sky, people everywhere.

The day seemed to drag on forever, circling in the back of my mind was the situation in Anchorage. I felt for Marks girlfriend and her son. I didn't have much sympathy for Mark, he knew what he was doing, and he knew the price.

Getting back to our room I noticed the message light on our phone was blinking, I called the front desk and got the message. It was from Marks girlfriend, it read please call as soon as possible. I dialed the front desk and asked them place a call to the United States. The phone rang only once and the voice on the other end was that of a man, I asked for Marks girlfriend and was told she had been arrested. I asked who he was and he stated he was with the Bureau of Narcotics. He asked me who I was and I told him, I said I was a personal friend of the couple and I wanted to find out what had happened, he refused to give me any details but told me that they both were housed in the Anchorage jail. I asked if there had been a bail hearing and he said that her bail was set, but Marks was being determined. By the time I was able to get information is was late in the day and much later in Alaska. I would have to wait until morning.

The night proved to be restless, so many thoughts running through my head, it was impossible to sleep. Early the next morning I received a call from Marks girlfriend, she had posted bail and was home.

We had just a few more hours in Hong Kong, so we decided to just take our time packing and relax before our flight home. I suggested to my wife that we get off in Hawaii and spend some time on the beach. It wasn't a hard decision. My wife had a very good friend that lived on Maui and we could just do the tourist thing and visit.

Stepping off the plane in Maui I felt a sense of relief, although Taiwan and China were interesting I just felt good to be back on familiar soil. The sun felt good on my face and the air was fresh and clean. My wife's friend met us at the airport with the traditional lei and drove us to our beachfront hotel. I checked in and my wife and her friend went to the patio restaurant for some lunch. As soon as I got to our room I opened the sliding glass door that led to a small balcony, I had a view of Diamond Head and the breeze from the ocean provided a soothing fresh feeling. I called Marks girlfriend in Anchorage to get an update.

She answered the phone and I could tell she was still very upset. She said Marks bail had been set at $100,000.00 she then asked me if I could help him get out. I said I would have to ask my wife and I would get back to her in a few hours, with that we said goodbye. I found my way down to the restaurant and met my wife and her friend. They had found a

small little table that sat under a beautiful palm tree facing the ocean. I sat down and ordered a fruit plate and an iced tea. For the first time in a couple of weeks I actually felt relaxed. I told my wife that I had called Alaska and we needed to talk, looking at me she just smiled and said "just do what you think is right."

The lunch was great and the company was even better, my wife's friend was involved in all sorts of things on the island and invited us to an out door concert later in the evening; we accepted and left for our room. I was sitting on the balcony and my wife stood in the door and asked me what I had decided to do. I paused for a minute and said I was going to post bail for Mark, it would be $10,000.00 or ten percent of the bail amount. I knew he was good for the money and would give it back to me the minute he was released. My only fear was that the powers that be would question my involvement. That thought passed quickly because I knew that I would be able to weather any questions that might arise. Mark had become a friend and I keep my word. I called

Marks girlfriend and said I would bail him out, I just needed a name of the bail bondsman and I could make arrangements to wire the money as soon as possible. She thanked me and said she would call me as soon as she had the information I had requested.

The evening was a beautiful and the concert took place in an outdoor amphitheater. There were chairs available but we chose to put a blanket on the small hillside just above the seating area. The scents of the orchids in the garden were wonderful and the palm trees seemed to sway with the music. I just lay there on my back and starred at the stars, now and then closing my eyes and counting my blessings.

The next morning I made arrangements to have my bank wire the money to a bondsman in Anchorage. I called Marks girlfriend and told her that it all should be done by noon her time and to have Mark call me when he got out, she said she would and thanked me again for my help.

My wife and I had planned to spend the day on the beach. We found two lounge chairs near the waters edge and just let the ocean breeze soothe our souls. The day lingered on and we just enjoyed all the sights and sounds of the Big Island. When we decided to call it a beach day, we returned to our room to shower and clean up for dinner. We had promised to meet my wife's friend for a Luau, I'm normally not one who attends these types of gatherings, but this time I agreed. It was a beautiful evening and the luau was taking place on the beach. It had Hawaiian dancers in traditional costumes, Hula dancers performed on stage and all in all it was very pleasant. I jokingly told my wife she might want to learn the hula, with that she just smiled and said she would if I would. Well that wasn't going to happen, so I guess she got off the hook.

It was getting late and I was tired, I think I had baked in the sun a little too long, so I excused myself. I said goodbye. My wife said she and her friend were going to go back to her house and catch up on old times. I bid them a farewell and returned to my room. It didn't take me long before I fell asleep.

My sleep was disturbed by the phone. It was Mark, he couldn't thank me enough for arranging his freedom, I assured him it was ok and just hoped he was ok. Mark said he would wire the money to my bank the next day, I told him that would be fine, and I wasn't worried.

There was a long pause on his end, I asked him what was wrong, he spoke softly and asked me for another favor, I was about out of favors, but I asked him what he needed. His answer surprised me. He said he would like me to come to Anchorage as soon as I could. I could hear a panic in his voice. I said I would talk to my wife, he then stated that he would pay for everything and not to worry about the money. I told him it wasn't about the money, but told him if I was going to come, he indeed would pay. He laughed; I sensed a relief in his voice. We said goodbye, he thanked me again.

I looked around the room and saw that my wife was not back yet, so my talk with her would have to wait. I tried to fall asleep again but just tossed and turned, my mind was recalling Marks conversation. Why did he need me in Anchorage for? What was it he thought I could do for him?

⋏

The next morning I ordered room service, for some reason Hawaiian coffee always seemed the best way to start my morning. I snuck out of the room and let my wife sleep. I found the beach all but deserted, just a few workers straightening the beach chairs, raking the white sand, making the beach pristine for the tourists. I walked near the waters edge, letting the warm Pacific Ocean wash over my feet. As I walked, I turned and noticed that all my footsteps had been washed away behind me. It was like I hadn't been there at all. It was a touch of reality.

I got back to our room some time later, my wife was up and getting dressed for the beach. I said I needed to talk to her, and proceeded to tell her about last nights conversation with Mark. She too was puzzled, why would he want me to come to Alaska. I said I would talk to him later and decide then. She mentioned that she and her friend were going to fly over to the island of Kona today and visit some people she knew there. They were all interested in some music thing that was going on. I told her that was great and that I would just hang out on the beach and catch up on my reading. She left around noon and I found myself a nice spot on the beach in front of the hotel, just far enough away from the noise but close enough for lunch. I ordered a large iced tea and settled in for a relaxing day.

The day just seemed to slip into evening. I had been on the beach almost four hours, and I had dozed off several times. I found myself thinking about Mark, his girlfriend and her son. I just couldn't get them out of my mind.

My wife arrived back at the hotel around 6:30 and we went down to the patio restaurant to have a light dinner. I asked her how her day had been and she talked about a new music school on Kona, she and her friend had visited. She was excited about the prospect of the native Hawaiian children being able to learn music from their culture. We talked about making plans to return to Oregon.

She than asked me if I had given anymore thought about going to Alaska to visit Mark. I told her of my concern for his girlfriend and her son. She suggested that I go and see what I could do. I called Mark and told him that I would be up as soon as we returned to Oregon, maybe about a week or so. He agreed and that was that.

After another day on the island my wife and I reluctantly decided that it was time to go home. We had made plans to go to dinner at our friend's home that evening, so we put making our reservations on hold until tomorrow.

The road to the north side of the island was winding and narrow, the beach on one side and beautiful landscaped hillside homes on the other. As we proceeded along we could see small turnoffs where you could stop to take pictures or watch the sunsets. Looking out toward the ocean we could see surfers lined up waiting for the perfect wave. My wife commented, "I wish I could live here". I didn't give it much thought, I just agreed as a good husband would. Arriving at our friends house found us walking through an arbor covered with beautiful fragrant flowers, entering the house was like entering an arboretum, flowers of all shapes and sizes and colors. The house was a small cottage nestled among a lush garden; a small pond lay in the center of a patio off the kitchen, with multi colored coy fish swimming under lily pads that created shade for the pond. The windows and doors were all open letting the trade winds blow throughout the cottage. Our

hostess greeted us and escorted us to the patio where she had prepared a pitcher of iced tea. We sat at a small round table that faced the beautiful garden. I could tell my wife had fallen in love with Hawaii. It was going to be hard to get her to leave.

The conversation turned toward how my wife had always wanted to live here. Our friend said that the main house on the grounds where her cottage was located was for lease. It was so well hidden we hadn't even seen it as we arrived. She didn't know how much they wanted for the lease, she went on to say the house was large and furnished. She would make a call if we were serious. I could see in my wife's eyes that she was serious, so that meant I was. We nodded at each other and told our friend to make the call.

It didn't take long for the owner of the main house to call back; she lived in San Francisco and wanted to lease the house for a year. I wasn't keen on leasing for a year, but my wife was ok with it. My wife and she talked for sometime, I could tell this was getting close after some small talk my wife hung up the phone. As she turned to me I could see that this was a done deal in her mind. I asked her when we could see the house and she said right now. We proceed up a long narrow path that led from the cottage to the main house. Arriving at the front of the house I could see a beautiful home perched in a hill overlooking the Pacific Ocean. The deck wrapped around the entire house. Full picture windows gleamed as the sunset was reflected back to the sea.

Upon entering the house it was plain to see why my wife was excited. The house was fully furnished in every way. The massive living room opened to the deck, the glass walls slid completely open to give the feeling of no walls at all. The bathrooms were large and had separate showers with a sunken tub in the master. The master bedroom was almost as large as the living room; the bed was placed so you could be awakened by the morning sun. Its glass walls also retracted. There was no doubt that we were going to live here for awhile. The next day found us signing the year lease.

We checked out of the hotel and immediately moved in to our house. We only needed a few supplies and it didn't take long to settle in. My wife and I agreed I needed to go back to Oregon and take care of some business. I needed to transfer money to a bank in Hawaii, I needed to make arrangements to have one of our cars shipped over and also find someone who could take care of the Oregon house. I knew my wife would be fine, she had her friend and she had already become interested in several projects.

My wife took me to the airport and we said our goodbyes. The flight to Portland was uneventful; I had acquired enough frequent flyer miles to upgrade to first class. This made the flight more comfortable. I arrived in Portland in the early afternoon, to no surprise it was pouring down rain. My friend picked me up in my car and we drove to my house on the coast. It was good to be home, I loved the Oregon coast, especially in a big storm. I built a fire and turned the lights down low, I sat in front of the fire and listened to the storm, I fell asleep sitting in my old leather chair. The phone brought me back to life, it was my wife checking to see if I had arrived ok, we chatted for awhile and said goodnight.

It was nice to sleep in my own bed, the wind and the rain made my nights sleep even better. I got up around 9:30 a.m. which was sleeping in for me. I made my way downstairs and made some Kona coffee that I had brought back from Hawaii. Sitting in the kitchen I could see the storm had cleared and the sun was breaking through the clouds. I thought to myself, what a great day. I had several things I needed to do around the house, we hadn't been home in over a month, mail had to be read, bills had to be paid and calls returned. This took up the better part of the day, I finally had a chance to sit down and relax, it was about 6:30 when the phone rang, and I thought it would my wife, but to my surprise it was Mark, he wanted to know if I could come to Alaska in the next few days. I finally asked him what was so important that I needed to be there. He said he was meeting with his attorney and they were going to go over his defense, again I asked him why he needed me I said "what defense, you're guilty; you got caught with a trunk full of illegal shit". He replied "my attorney would like to meet you and maybe you can be a character witness." I told Mark that I would have to think about it. I then asked him who he had retained as his attorney, his answer shocked me. "Phillip Weidner" he said, I just sat there stunned, and I made him repeat it one more time. "Do you know him?" I said "yes I know him". I then asked him why Weidner, he replied that his own attorney Bill Bryson had recommended Weidner. I again told Mark that I would have to see if I could make it.

I told him I would get back to him in a few days, and with that said I goodbye and hung up the phone. Still stunned my mind began to put together a gruesome puzzle.

It was becoming clear that Mark was involved in something bigger than just a few polar bear skins and ivory. I needed to go to Alaska and see how deep he was in and what else he had done. Phillip Weidner was known in certain circles as the "drug lawyer" in Alaska. He didn't come cheap.

I called my wife and told her of Mark's phone call, I told her I needed to go to Alaska, there was some hesitation in her voice, but she told me to go ahead and go. I told her that I would fly from Anchorage to Hawaii when I was done visiting Mark.

I called Mark and told him I would be there in two days, I had more things I needed to do here at home. I said I would get back to him with my flight numbers. I finished my business at home and packed for Alaska. It was early in the month of February 1987, and Anchorage temperature was in the low 20's and I was totally unprepared for the cold weather clothing wise. I bought some warm clothes for the trip, and called Mark with my flight numbers, I would arrive tomorrow.

I was somewhat worried about seeing Phillip Weidner again, although we had never spoken, the encounters we had at the first Investor trial left me wondering about his involvement with Mark. His continued insistence that the Investor murders were over drugs, and that it was a "mafia hit" kept coming back to me. I tried not to think about it.

Mark met me at the Airport in Anchorage, I told him I had made reservations at the Captain Cook Hotel, and he insisted that I stay with him and his girlfriend, so we drove to their house. He lived in a nice suburb of Anchorage. As we pulled up to his house I could see nothing out of the ordinary, it was a nice house at the end of the short street in a quiet neighborhood. A boat was parked in the driveway, and a snowmobile on a trailer next to it. Just the usual Alaska toys.

Greeting me at the door was Marks girlfriend, she said she was headed to work and would see us later. She thanked me for coming and left. I could hear a noise upstairs and was soon to meet her son. He was as a typical young boy, more interested in what was for dinner than meeting me? He said "hello" when Mark introduced us, then ran off to his room. I was shown the guest room and put my bags on the bed. Mark then made some coffee, not Kona, but pretty good coffee.

Mark didn't waste any time explaining why I was here. He said that Phillip Weidner has turned him back over to his regular attorney Bill Bryson. He stated that Weidner thought that Bryson could handle his case without much trouble. I thought to myself this was a bit strange, but didn't let Mark know of my suspicions.

Mark went on to say that he thought the state "didn't have a case that they had set him up." I just sat there and listened, I couldn't get a word in anyway, so I listened. Mark was so out of touch with what was happening that is was scary, he wasn't facing the reality that they had him and he was going to jail. It just wasn't going to happen to him. Finally Mark took a breath and got up to pour us some more coffee. I took this opportunity to speak to the issues he had just brought up. First I asked Mark "did you do what they say you did?" did you have the polar bear skins? Did you have the ivory? Did you have the cash and cocaine?' Mark looked at me and with some hesitation said "yes." I then said "then how can you say they set you up?" Mark paused and said "well they didn't get it all." I knew immediately this was not going to end here.

It was getting late and I was tired, I needed to call my wife and tell her I had arrived safely, and get some sleep. I told Mark that I was going to call it a night and would see him in the morning.

The morning was a typical winter morning in Anchorage, dark and cold. Mark's girlfriend had already started her day, up early to take her son to school; she had already made coffee and started breakfast. I wondered out of the bedroom and she greeted me with a cheerful good morning. I mumbled something and she handed me a cup of coffee. Looking around I could see that Mark had already left the house. I asked her about his whereabouts, she said "he doesn't tell me where he goes, he just leaves the same time everyday".

We talked a lot about what had happened. She shared that she had never been so scared and was concerned about her son. I tried to reassure her that it was going to be ok. I looked at the clock and it was already 9:30, I excused myself and headed for the shower. When I returned from the shower Mark was in the kitchen. I could sense the mood was cold and tense. Mark told me that we had an appointment in about an hour with his attorney. I went to my bedroom and started to get dressed, I could hear Mark and his girlfriend trying to keep their voices low, but I could hear an argument. The argument seemed to be about the situation that Mark had put her in. She was saying she could loose her son as well as her job because of their arrest. Marks reply took me by surprise. He said "I'm not going to jail, I'll get out of here before that happens, and I'll leave you here." I could see this wasn't going to turn out well. Marks ego was going to get him in deep trouble.

I returned to the kitchen and the tension was palatable, I tried to lighten the mood by commenting on how dark it was outside at 11 a.m. and how dark it was in here, even with the lights on.

They both tried to force a laugh.

Mark said he would like me to come with him; he had to visit his attorney, after that he would show me around Anchorage. Once in the car I turned to Mark and said "what the fuck was that about?" Mark looked at me and said "she's just being a bitch, she asks too many questions."

I just smiled, "you better start treating her like gold, she can testify against you" I replied. "You have put her and her son in a bad situation and she's scared." She won't do anything like that, Mark said as we pulled into the parking lot of his attorney's office. When I approached the door I could see the name William Bryson etched on the door. As we entered the receptionist greeted Mark as if they were old friends, this seemed a little strange to me. I thought Mark had only known him a short time. Not having time to sort this out, we were ushered into Bryson's office. "Bill Bryson", he said as he stuck out his hand, and you are? "I'm Mike McGuire" I said as he pointed to two chairs in front of his desk. We sat down and he asked Mark how things were going. Mark said" I'm getting things squared away." Again I wondered what Mark was referring to.

The conversation quickly turned to the case. Mark said that he wanted a jury trial and Bryson said "I don't recommend that Mark".

Bryson went on to say "the evidence in overwhelming, they have had you under surveillance for over a year." Mark once again denied any involvement. Bryson then had us listen to a few tapes that he was given from the district attorney in his discovery motion. There were boxes of tapes as well as videos of Mark meeting with undercover agents from Fish and Game. In my opinion Mark was fucked.

After listening for about thirty minutes, I had heard all I needed to. I got up and went outside. Mark followed me out and asked me "what do you think?" I said I think you should listen to you attorney, I'm sure you're paying him big bucks." Mark smiled and said "thank you for reminding me" with that Mark opened the trunk of his car and took out a brown paper bag. As we walked back into the office I saw Mark hand the bag to the receptionist. I shook Bryson's hand and thanked him for his help with Mark. He looked me in the eye and said "please talk him into a trail by Judge, a jury will hang him." I thought this was strange, but let it pass. I knew that Mark would do what he wanted, I knew Mark well enough to know that nobody could change his mind.

Once in the car I could tell that Mark was upset, he started ranting about the fucking cops and how he had been set up. Not taking any responsibility for any of his actions. I interrupted" what was in the bag you handed to the receptionist." "Twenty five thousand dollars and some other goodies" he replied. "Are you a complete idiot" I asked. "You can bet your ass the cops are watching your every move." "I thought you were smarter than this." Mark just looked at me with a bewildered look. I thought to myself, this is the first time in his life he has had any run in with the law, and that explains his behavior.

I mentioned to him we should get some coffee and talk about this. He agreed and we headed out of town to a coffee shop he knew about.

We asked for a table away from the crowd. Once seated I asked Mark what was really bothering him? He paused, and then said "I have been dealing drugs for over fifteen years, and they bust me for some fucking skins and Ivory. I can't believe how stupid I was." He went on to say I still have "a lot of product left and I need to get rid of it." I quickly said "I don't want to know." "I'm not going to get involved in your business and I don't like you even thinking I will help you with this shit." Mark could see I was serious and apologized. He said he was scared and just felt alone. I said" you made your choices and now you get to pay the price." "You need to get rid of whatever you have and keep a low profile, and I don't want to know anything." I also re-emphasized that he needed to follow his attorney's direction.

I asked Mark why he had product in the house. It just didn't seem to fit. He responded that what they had found was going to be delivered the next morning, "I just got sloppy" he said. I asked him where we were going and he told me "just wait and see". It seemed like we were driving a long time, we finally pulled into an old run down trailer park. I asked Mark what we were doing here again he said" you'll see". I asked him where we were and he said it's called "Spenard, it's where all the strip joints and massage parlors are," I said "I'm not in the mood for a massage" he just laughed. The car pulled to a stop in front of an old broken down trailer. The snow was three feet deep all around the trailer. Parked alongside was an old pickup truck. At one time it had been painted green, now it was a faded shade of yellow, the windows of the trailer were covered with curtains made from bath towels blocking any view from the street. Mark fiddled with a set of keys and found the one that opened the front door. I asked him what the hell this is. He said "this is where I come; this is where I do my business." I once again felt very uneasy, Mark showed me several items that he had collected over the years, gold nuggets from the Yukon Territory, scrimshaw ivory pieces, and several pieces of native art. I knew the items were valuable and asked him why he kept them here? He said it was safe and he had other places for really valuable things.

I said "I feel very uneasy here and we should get out of here." I think he was trying to show me how successful he had been, successful in a dark and dangerous world. It seemed that Mark was trying to impress me, or maybe trying to justify his existence. Either way I wasn't comfortable.

⋌

Arriving back at Marks house, we found his girlfriend and her son in the kitchen doing homework. I could see she was tired and this was her night off. I suggested we go out to dinner, it would be my treat. She called a babysitter and we made plans for the evening.

The three of us were just about to leave when Mark received a phone call. I couldn't hear all of the conversation but by the reaction of Mark I could tell it was important. When he returned he said that we should go without him and he would meet up with us later. Mark's girlfriend told him where we would be, and we went our separate ways. I was somewhat relieved to be spending some time with her, I knew something was wrong and I hoped she would talk to me about it.

We found a Mexican restaurant that appeared to be the "hot spot", its décor was intensely Mexican, and it was very crowded and very noisy. We had to wait several minutes before being seated, once seated we took our time ordering. I asked her if we should wait until Mark arrived and she said "don't count on that". I immediately got her drift; he probably wasn't going to show. We chatted about her job her son and eventually got around to the current situation. We ordered and continued to talk. She said that Mark had become very distant, he had become verbally abusive and she was scared for her and her son.

I listened carefully trying not to interrupt her. Once she was finished I asked her "did you know that there were drugs in the house?" She said "absolutely not". I believed her. She asked me what the lawyer had said today. I told her that he had told Mark to have his case tried by a Judge and not a jury. She then asked me what I thought. I told her that they had Mark on tape selling Polar Bear skins and Ivory. They had him under surveillance for over a year. He was part of a large sting. I then went on to say that I believed they had no idea he had been selling cocaine. She said to me "he's the biggest dealer in Alaska, and has been for years." "He has property in Oregon where he grows marijuana." "He brings in 20 to 30 kilo's of cocaine at a time. He's tied into some real dangerous people. Even the Columbians here are afraid of him. He has connections that allow him access to the pipeline." She went on to say" he has money stashed all over this town." Trying not to look surprised, I changed the subject. I asked her what she was going to do. Her response was somewhat surprising. She told me that she didn't have enough money to move and would be stuck here if Mark goes to prison. She said she wanted to leave Alaska and move back to Seattle. Her family lives there and she would be able to transfer to a Seattle base. I found it very interesting that she felt so imprisoned. Mark had no concern about her welfare. I told her if she needed to leave I would make sure that she had the means to do so. I could see her relief and just gave her a reassuring smile. To no surprise Mark failed to show, but we had a very nice dinner and headed home about 9:30. Arriving at the house we noticed that Marks car wasn't there yet. I paid the babysitter and we built a fire in the living room fireplace and sat down for some coffee. An hour passed and we heard a car pull in the driveway. It was Mark, as he came through the door he was already apologizing, saying that his meeting had taken longer than expected. He asked if we had enjoyed our dinner date. I could sense a tone of voice that was a bit sarcastic; his insinuation that we had "enjoyed" our date took me by surprise. I found myself angry at his thought that his girlfriend and I had more than dinner. "You're one sick fuck I said to him." "Don't ever go that direction with me". With that I got up and went to my room to pack. He followed and again was apologetic. He could see that I was not going to play his fucked up game. I told him to take me to the hotel, I was not going to stay and take his shit any longer. I told him that he was out of control and I didn't want to be involved. I also told him that if anything happened to his girlfriend or her son I would personally see to it that he paid. He knew I was serious and didn't question me.

I said my goodbyes to his girlfriend and reminded her that my wife and I were available to her anytime she needed us.

Mark drove me to the hotel; the silence was palatable on the way there. Finally Mark spoke, "will you come to my trial?" he asked. I thought to myself, what balls, one minute he accuses me of fucking his girlfriend, the next he wants my support at his trial. This man was a sociopath, no guilt, no remorse, just self will run riot. I told him I would think about it, but it wouldn't be for him. He knew I was pissed, so he just let it go.

I didn't see Mark again for several months. He did call me several times just to keep me informed. I talked to his girlfriend several times and assured her that it was all going to be ok.

It was sometime in May or June of 1998 that Mark called again. This time he was very humble. He asked if my wife and I could come to Alaska in July for his sentencing. He had decided to listen to his attorney and go before a judge. He said he had made a plea deal. I hesitated for awhile before answering. I asked him what plans had been made for his girlfriend and her son. He stated that they were part of the plea agreement. I thought to myself this doesn't sound like the Mark I know, this just didn't feel right. I said I would ask my wife what she thought and get back to him.

I mentioned this call to my wife; she thought a minute and suggested that we drive from Oregon to Alaska in our Motor home. I said that I would have to go to Oregon and prepare for the trip. We hadn't used the RV in over a year and it would need some preparation. After some thought, I agreed it would be a great trip. The Islands had been great, and we had found some special memories. The lease would be up soon and after all Oregon was still home. I called Mark back and told him of our plans. He was excited and said he would pay for whatever expenses we would incur.

The trip to Alaska from Oregon by way of the Alcan Highway (Alaska Canadian Hwy) would take us ten days driving at a nice pace. We would leave Oregon on July 1st. With that date set we needed to get busy. I would fly back to Oregon and get everything ready. I would pick my wife up in Seattle and we would head north. I felt a little excited, and was looking forward to the adventure. Little did I know at the time that this trip would change my life forever.

July came faster that I expected. I had been in Oregon a month, but time had flown by. All was ready, the motor home was all set to go, the house was secured and I was off to Seattle to pick up my wife and start a new journey. The drive to Alaska would take us through some of the most spectacular country I have ever seen. It started at the Canadian border. My wife and I decided to turn right at the border and proceed to Harrison Hot Springs. If there is a natural Hot Springs my wife has to soak in it. That's all there is to it. It wasn't that far off the beaten track so it was not a big deal. After all this was supposed to be an adventure. We have never found much adventure staying on the main road anyway. I think that holds true in all areas of life. We spent a day just soaking in the springs and taking in the natural beauty. We would get an early start the next morning.

From Harrison Hot Springs we traveled north staying the night in Williams Lake. This drive took us through several provincial state parks, the beauty was ever changing. The area around Williams Lake was beautiful and forested. We found a beautiful park next to the lake and had a star filled night. The sky was clear and the heaven's put on a glorious light show just for us. Shooting star's dotted the night sky leaving bright fiery trails behind them as they seemed to fall to earth all around us. This was indeed an adventure I would hold dear for many years to come.

The next day found us bound for Prince George British Columbia. It would be a two hundred mile drive and in the Motor home it would take six hours. We arrived in Prince George about 4:30 pm. We unhooked our car and did some shopping. Wanting to explore my wife took the car and proceeded to just drive around the city. I stayed with the Motor home and did some cleaning and prepared dinner. The next day we started early. This days drive would take us easterly through some beautiful forests, it seemed like every time we passed through a beautiful forest we would come upon a lake that matched. The waters were clear and cold, the shorelines kissed the trees and the pristine surroundings seemed uncluttered by anything human. We had our pick of campgrounds and choose one near Burns Lake. Getting an early start the next day was important. We were going to try to make it to the Yukon Territory by tomorrow evening. Watson Lake was going to be our goal. Watson Lake was the first city in the Yukon Territory. It didn't come any too soon. The trip seemed like it was all up hill and it took us over twelve hours. There isn't much in Watson Lake but we found a campground and hooked up for the night. I had to do some repair to the Motor home, the rough road had managed to loosen some bolts on the awning and I wanted to just give it an overall inspection. I needed to check under the hood and make sure all was well. For from now on our trip would take us through some sparsely populated areas and services would be minimal.

The next day found us choosing whether we should go west over to Whitehorse or north to Ross River either way we were going to have to pass over the Pelley Mountains. We decided to go north and make it to Ross River. We thought we could return through Whitehorse. Either way we definitely wanted to visit Whitehorse. The history of the Gold Rush and the Yukon riverboats had always been something I wanted to see. Whitehorse was the hub for all this history. We would see it on the return trip. This way we would be able to take our time. Marks sentencing was going to be on the 10th of July so we needed to make better time. We arrived in Ross River about 8:30 the evening of July 4th and settled in. Ross River was a small town with only a gas station that also contained a small grocery and the post office. We stocked up on snacks and spent the evening writing post cards we had acquired along the way. The next day we would head north to Dawson. Dawson played an important role during the Gold Rush days. Many prospectors stopped here on their way to the gold fields. Much to our surprise it also had a wonderful Hot Springs to my wife's delight. We decided to spend a full day here and catch our breath.

The Yukon Territory is the one of the most beautiful places on earth. The unspoiled beauty, the ruggedness and the feeling of history abounds. The people here are self sustaining warm and friendly. Several times we had to stop to let a bear or moose cross the road. Time just seemed to stand still. We found ourselves traveling several miles without seeing anyone or anything that resembled a community. Sometimes we would see a light way off in the distance in the middle of nowhere. The road had become rough and washboard like, which made the ride jarring a slow. Travel was slow but the scenery made up for the inconvience. We were going to be back in Alaska the next day and probably make it to Anchorage the day after that.

The rest of the trip seemed uneventful. Maybe it was the reality of what lay ahead or maybe we were just tired. Arriving in Anchorage we were met by Mark somewhere outside the city limits. We didn't know Anchorage that well and maneurving the Motor home in city traffic wasn't my idea of fun. Mark met us and we followed him to his house where we were able to park. As we pulled in his driveway we were met by his girlfriend and her son. They both seemed glad to see us. Mark informed us that his sentencing had been moved up to tomorrow. He had not been able to reach us so we had no idea. At least we made in time. I kind of felt it was the way it was supposed to be.

I really didn't want to spend a lot of time with him before the sentencing day anyway. We made plans to have dinner together and my wife and I went back to the Motor home to clean up. My wife immediately asked me if I had felt the same tension as she had felt. I agreed that it seemed tense. She suggested that maybe she should try to get the girlfriend aside and see if she was ok. I agreed and we made plans to do so. I noticed that the toys, the boat and snowmobile were gone; I also noticed the garage was empty. When Mark knocked on the door and came into the Motor home I asked him what he had done with the toys. He said his friend Bear had bought them, I asked him who Bear was, because I thought it was a strange name. He said that we would meet Bear tomorrow at the sentencing. With that my wife told Mark that she needed to go shopping and would like his girlfriend to go with her.

My wife and Marks girlfriend left for awhile and Mark and I were alone. The conversation turned to his plea agreement. I asked him what he had agreed too and did he have any idea what the sentence would be. He said that he had agreed to plead guilty possession 500 grams of cocaine, agreed to forfeit the money confiscated and pay $3.500 in fines and $1.500 in court costs and serve a minimum sentence. I asked him about the charges regarding the Polar Bear skins, and the Ivory tusks. He just smiled. I was later to find out that the department of Fish and Game was livid with this agreement. If Mark had been convicted in those areas he would have faced fifty years. Instead he pleaded guilty to three counts of trafficking in walrus ivory and polar bear hides. Mark had done something, he had turned on someone, who I didn't know but I was sure he had made a sweet deal. He went on to say that he would be given some time to put his affairs in order before going to prison after sentencing.

We changed the subject. I asked him what he had done to make sure his girlfriend was taken care of, his reply startled me. He said" I gave her some money". "I gave her five thousand dollars". I thought to myself, you asshole, she can bury you and all you give her is five grand, knowing full well he had hundreds of thousands stashed. I kind of hoped she would speak up, but I knew full well she was too scared to do so. I was just going to shut up; it's really none of my business.

My wife and Marks girlfriend returned home. My wife had purchased some gifts to send to her friends and some supplies for the trip home. After putting things away I asked her if she had a chance to talk to talk to his girlfriend. She said that she had talked briefly but the girl was too afraid to say much. She just said that she was going to move as soon as she could, she needed to get out of Alaska. She said that she was frightened and didn't want to stay here. My wife went on to say that

Marks girlfriend had asked us to stay with her for awhile after Mark left for prison. I said I would have to think about that for awhile.

We went to dinner that night and all seemed well on the outside. I could tell Mark was really nervous about tomorrow and his girlfriend was seemed anxious to get it over with as well, albeit for different reasons I supposed. During dinner we tried to talk of brighter subjects, I directed the conversation toward brighter days, trying to ease the tension, but it appeared to fall on deaf ears. So with dinner completed we excused ourselves and my wife and I went to our Motor home to retire for the night. Tomorrow was going to be a long stressful day and I was tired, not only from the drive but from the past few months of Mark and his drama. Sad to say but I was glad this was coming to an end. At least Mark would be away and safe and my wife and I would have fulfilled our promise to him and his girlfriend. The nights sleep was difficult, the sun seemed like it never went down. In July it never really gets dark in Anchorage, the sky remains light 24 hours a day. Just the opposite of when I visited last winter where it never really got light.

I think I would find it difficult to live here my wife said as she tried to close all the curtains. I would find it hard to stay awake during the winter. I would find it very depressing if I couldn't see the sun everyday she said. And just as hard if I couldn't get sleep in the summer because it was never really dark. I agreed and we tried to get some sleep.

The next day found us up having coffee around 6:30am. Mark rapped on our door and brought us some freshly baked blueberry muffins from the local bakery. It was plain to see he hadn't slept much the previous night. I asked him what time we needed to leave for court and he said we needed to leave by 9:30. He said he had to meet some people before then and would meet us there. I found this strange, but knowing Mark he was still cleaning up business and possibly even handing over his business to someone else even at this late date. Marks girlfriend had made arrangements for someone to take care of the little boy. I knew it was going to be hard for him to understand Mark leaving. But at least Mark would have a few weeks to settle him down and explain why he was leaving. Maybe it would be a lie, but it didn't matter. As long as the little boy was spared this ordeal.

My wife and I and Marks girlfriend left the house a little before 9:30. I let her drive our car so we wouldn't get lost. It took about twenty minutes to get to the courthouse and find a parking spot. When we arrived we saw Mark standing outside with several people. I asked his girlfriend who they were, she said that the two women were Marks mother and sister, the large man standing next to Mark was Bear Piereski, Marks friend and she added business associate. She went on to say that Piereski had something to do with the Labor Union but she wasn't sure what it was. She also said Mark took her to a fishing lodge that Bear owned on the Kenai Peninsula.

Mark spotted us as we were walking up to the courthouse, he waved us toward the group of people. When we arrived at the spot they were gathered, Mark introduced me to his Mother. She was a petite redhead, she was dressed in expensive clothes and she appeared somewhat aloof. Next his sister, she was nothing like her Mother, she was open and friendly, she appeared to be concerned for Mark and very supportive. Then I was introduced to Bear Piereski, his name suited him. He was a mountain of a man, impeccably dressed and tailored. He reached out his hand, a hand that seemed as large as a grizzley paw. I took it and we shook hands. He said that Mark had good things to say about me, with that I said responded "thank you". It was now almost ten, the time had come top go into the courthouse. Mark and his family went in first, my wife and Marks girlfriend went next and Bear and I followed. Once in the doors, Marks attorney Bill Bryson greeted us. He smiled and thanked me for coming, I introduced my wife and we all proceeded into the courtroom. Mark and his attorney stepped up to the defense table and sat down. My wife and I and Marks girlfriend sat a few rows back. His Mother and sister sat on the other side of the room, which at the time seemed strange to me. Bear sat directly behind us.

As the judge entered the room we all stood up at the request of the bailiff, once the Judge was seated we all sat down.

The court clerk called docket number 10951-006 State of Alaska versus Mark A Ward. Judge James Fitzgerold asked if all parties were present, Bill Bryson replied "the defense is ready". The district attorney replied "the state is ready your honor." With that the Judge Fitzgerold called the court to order.

Reading from a prepared document the judge asked if both parties were in agreement with the plea agreement. He looked directly at Mark and asked him "Mr. Hayward do you wave your rights to a jury trial and have you read and do you understand the agreement made with the district attorney?" Mark responded "yes your honor", his voice trembling as he spoke. Judge Fitzgerold then went on to pronounce sentence. "In the case of The State of Alaska versus Mark A Ward the state finds the defendant guilty." "The court herby sentences the defendant to five years in federal prison for possession of cocaine." The court also sentences the defendant to six months for each of the three counts of trafficking in polar bear hides and walrus ivory." These will be served concurrently with the first sentence, the defendant will forfeit any money found in his possession. The court orders the defendant to pay $3000.00 in restitution and $1,500.00 in court costs.

Mr. A Ward will be taken into custody immediately and will await transport to a federal facility." Bill Bryson rose from his chair and objected. "Your honor, we had an agreement that Mr. A Ward would be allowed time to put his affairs in order." "Mr. Bryson, I have been more than fair in this case. I'm not in total agreement with the deal the State made with your client, however I will honor it. It is my thought that your client has had more than sufficient time to put his affairs in order. So my ruling stands." Judge Fitzgerold then ordered the State Troopers to take Mark into custody. Mark rose from his chair and placed his hands behind his back, the Troopers handcuffed Mark and led him from the courtroom. As Mark was being led away I could hear a faint cry come from his sister. Marks girlfriend put her head on my wifes shoulder, and I turned to Bear Piereski and said "well that was a surprise." Mr. Piereski just nodded and turned to leave the courtroom. Once outside the family appeared stunned. Marks mother remained stoic, his sister was visibly upset. I approach them with my condolences. We said our goodbyes and turned to leave the courthouse. Bear Piereski nodded in my direction as if he wanted to speak to me privately. I approached him and as I did he reached into his suit jacket and pulled out an envelope and handed it to me. I asked him what it was for and he said Mark wanted me to have it. I just put it in my back pocket and didn't give it much thought. Bear then asked me if I liked to fish, I replied "hell yes" he then gave me a business card which read Big Bear

Lodge, Fishing at its best. He said that Mark had told him to invite me there for a week of salmon fishing. I thanked him and he said to call him anytime to make arrangements. I said I would, with that the big man walked away. I returned to my wife and Marks girlfriend. We then walked to the car and returned to Marks home.

Once there we just relaxed, it had been a tense day and we all were a little on edge. I suggested to Marks girlfriend that she pick up her son and we could go to dinner later.

Once alone with my wife I told her I was relieved that they had taken Mark into custody. I felt in my gut that he was ready to run; I knew he had the means and I knew how scared he was to go to prison. Maybe the judge caught wind of something my wife replied, maybe.

I felt in my back pocket and found the envelope Mark had given Bear to give to me. I opened it and to my surprise found a cashiers check made out to me for ten thousand dollars. I was shocked, I handed it to my wife in disbelief. I told he I was not about to keep it. I didn't want any of his drug money. We both agreed. We decided that we would give it to Marks girlfriend and her son. Knowing full well he hadn't left her anything. She could use it to make her move. When she arrived home we asked her in and gave her the check. I said I would cash it tomorrow for her. She just began sobbing and couldn't thank us enough. As far as I was concerned the ordeal was over.

Or was it?.

TRIAL II

Peel II would have another Judge. Juneau Superior Court Judge Walter L. "Bud" Carpeneti found himself in the middle of a cluster fuck to put it mildly. Carpeneti was appointed to the Peel trial on March 6, 1987 he was thrown a barrage of motions from both sides. Carpeneti was known for his scholarly approach to problems. Carpeneti was only 42 years old and a complete opposite of Judge Schulz. Carpeneti was known for his calm demeanor sometimes appearing almost unflappable. However this didn't make him a pushover for either side. Phillip Weidner and Mary Anne Henry would have to be on their best behavior in front of Judge Carpeneti. Carpeneti had spent some time in California working for the famous San Francisco lawyer Melvin Belli. Belli is a whole other story. I met Belli in Lake Chapala Mexico. Belli had run into some problems of his own. Belli was accused of shooting a woman in a plush club in Lake Chapala. He didn't do any jail time himself, he had one of his associates do the jail time for him.

The first issue that Judge Carpeneti faced was when and where to hold the second trial. The state wanted it to begin in July, the defense preferred September. Judge Carpeneti settled on November 16th, 1987. In June of 1987, Bob Blasco appeared before Judge Carpeneti with his argument that the Peel trial should not be held in Ketchikan. Phillip Weidner immediately countered that the state was trying to move the trial "because they got beat here in Ketchikan the first time"

Judge Carpeneti eventually ruled that the second trial would be held in Juneau, other considerations were Kenai, Kodiak, Seward and Sitka, and these were dismissed because Judge Carpeneti said they lacked adequate facilities. Weidner opposed the change of venue. Carpeneti turned him away. Judge Carpeneti had noted that he had received over 100 motions since his appointment to the trial. Judge Carpeneti made a ruling that pretty much set the tone of the upcoming trial.

"Barring a discovery of new facts, an intervening change in the law or a clearly erroneous ruling, both sides could forget about changing the law of the case."

The stage was set. Peel II was about to begin.

Fourteen months after his mistrial, the way had been cleared for John Peel to face another jury in his second trial on murder and arson. Jury selection took almost two months with both sides filing motions, many of which challenged prospective jurors.

Judge Carpeneti swore in the jury of twelve men and women and six alternates. He read them their instructions. "The jury system depends on honesty and integrity of each juror," he stated. He carefully reminded them that John Peel "begins with a clean slate." With that the jury was dismissed the jury for the day.

Phillip Weidner immediately began his antics. On the eve of opening statements, he filed another motion. This one asked to cross examine police officers regarding their failure to adequately investigate other suspects. Again he wanted to raise the issue that the murders were drug related. Weidner had again wanted his super conspiracy theory brought to the forefront. Weidner went on to say that even Judge Schulz had allowed him to question the police as to their failure to investigate other suspects. He stated that "there were statements to the effect that other suspects actually committed the crime."

Judge Carpeneti was not impressed; he wasn't buying the other suspect theory.

It was Friday January 15th, 1988 when the second trial actually began. The federal courthouse in Juneau was spacious; the actual courtroom was twice the size of the Ketchikan courtroom. As the trial began the courtroom was packed. Judge Carpeneti had moved the trial to a larger courtroom to accommodate the expected number of spectators. It wasn't long before Juneau had lost interest, the spectators thinned daily, however the front of the courtroom was still crowded, it was crowded with exhibits, scale models of the scene, as well as the complete records of the first trial. These were contained in dozens of banker's boxes. This display was intentional; both sides wanted the jury to see that the volume of paper this they thought would allow their arguments to prevail.

Mary Anne Henry's opening statement began where her first one had stopped. She stated "one shot fired from a gun held by John Peel, started what has been called the "Investor tragedy"

She went on to say that "The State can't tell you why that first shot was fired," thus acknowledging that the State could not come up with a motive for the murders. She went on to admit the failures of the police, at one point in her opening statement she stated "the troopers made one critical mistake that affected the way the investigation was conducted for an entire year." That mistake was their false assumption that John Peel had been eliminated as a suspect. This opening statement was far better than her first one that she gave almost two years earlier; it was free of unnecessary rhetoric and much more to the point. Why wouldn't it be, she had plenty of time to hone her skills.

Mary Anne Henry went on to discuss the "new evidence" her team had developed. She announced that all eight people aboard the Investor had been "positively identified," including Dean Moon. In the first trial it was argued that Dean Moon had not been identified, reports that Moon had been spotted in San Francisco were a strong argument for the defense. Another point in her opening statement in Peel II, focused on a statement that John Peel had confessed to the murders in 1983.

This new evidence came from statements of two brothers to whom he made the confession. Henry went on to tell the jury that that the two brothers would tell them in their own words that John Peel had confessed to killing Mark Coulthurst and Dean Moon.

The following day would be Phillip Weidner's turn. He arrived fully prepared to tear apart Mary Anne Henry's opening statement. His assistant Josef Princiotta, set out eight wooden easels, each containing a portion of a time line leading from the murders aboard the Investor, each easel was characterized with bold almost slanderous captions. Weidners opening statement like Henry's, was similar to his first opening statement in the first trial. He emphasized that John Peel was the "innocent victim of overzealous police efforts to solve a gruesome crime." As his opening statement continued, it would become clear that Weidner had no intention of foregoing his aggressive approach; in fact it appeared he would be more aggressive this time around.

As Weidner approached the end of his opening statement, it suddenly became clear that he was once again going after Larry Demmert Jr. with complete abandon. He referred to Larry as the state's "star witness."

Three of the easels contained a huge placards.

The first one read "STATE LIES AND THREATENS LARRY DEMMERT/RESULT---DREAMS."

The second placard read "DEMMERT GIVES TESTIMONY WHICH REQUIRES PERJURY IMMUNITY."

The third read "LARRY DEMMERT SCARED AND INFLUENCED BY HYPNOTIC DRUGS, AND THE THREAT OF JAIL. FLIP-FLOPS ON HIS STORY. *SUDDENLY* REMEMBERS JOHN PEEL."

As the trial approached the second month, many of the same witnesses testified and pretty much said the same thing as in the first trial. Testimony from a new witness that the state declared a "major witness" was delayed by an order from Judge Carpoletti. It seemed that a new witness had suddenly come forward. This witness also claimed to have heard John Peel confess to the murders during the summer of 1983. He would corroborate the testimony of the two other witnesses who had heard Peel's admission to the Investor murders. The state immediately sent Trooper Stogsdill to interview the witness. The first of the two brothers took the stand on Tuesday, February 23rd. he said he had met John Peel in 1983, while fishing near Kodiak, Alaska. The witness said he was playing cribbage with John Peel and mentioned having seen the burnt out wreckage of the Investor while passing through Craig in 1982. The witness went on to say he had hoped the murderer was arrested and executed for the crimes.

The witness went on to say that "John looked at me and said. " I did it. I killed them," the witness then added that "he kind of had a weird smile," and named Mark Coulthurst and Dean Moon among his victims. When asked why he hadn't come forward earlier, the witness stated that his father "told me to keep my mouth shut."

Later in the day the second brother took the stand. He pretty much said the same thing his brother had said in his testimony. There was one exception the witness said that John Peel "said he killed some people in Craig." "He said the Investor was the name of the boat. He burned it up." The witness said that Peel said it only once.

The state called several more witnesses, some had to be deemed hostile, and their testimony was less that forthcoming. It appeared that several witnesses from the first trial were tired of all the attention, all the badgering and most of all the time it had taken out of their lives.

Larry Demmert took the stand on March 17th; the prosecution strategy was to keep Larry's testimony as short as possible. This time Bob Blasco questioned Larry, his questioning only lasting thirty five minutes. His questioning only directed toward what Larry had seen and heard the night of the murders and the following morning. Blasco wanted Larry to testify that he had heard a scream and seen John Peel on the dock with a rifle. They wanted to avoid any questions that would open the door for Weidner on cross examination to bring up drugs or the first grand jury testimony. The wanted at all costs to avoid any unnecessary problems. The state was so concerned about a possible misdirection of testimony that they had taken every precaution they could think of.

The state wanted to make sure that any cross examination of Larry Demmert would not bring up any use of the term "addiction, being addicted, being an addict or abusing any drug." Belasco said that "the jury would most likely infer a bad connotation from the use of those terms."

The court affirmed the prosecution's position on references to addiction.

Phillip Weidner was not allowed to use the term "addict" or "addiction" or any similar words when questioning Larry Demmert.

For the better part of Demmert's first half hour on the stand Bob Blasco managed to keep Larry out of trouble. Larry remained calm and his testimony pointed directly at John Peel's guilt. Blasco asked John Peel's former skipper what he'd seen on Monday morning as the investor backed away from the float in Craig. Blasco wanted to know which of the Investor's lines had been untied by the person Demmert described as a "shadowy figure." Larry said he didn't know.

Blasco repeated the question, and Larry answered "I don,t know" once again.

At this point Weidner demanded the jury be excused; this had been an on going routine for Weidner. It seemed at times that the jury was out of the courtroom more than it was in. Weidner objected to Blasco's question, stating it was "improper" further stating that Larry had not testified that John Peel was on the Investor as it drifted away from the dock. As was Weidner's routine he asked for a mistrial. Judge Carpeneti routine had become taking Weidner's requests under advisement.

Cross examination found Phillip Weidner once again blasting Larry regarding his "inconsistent testimony." Weidner eventually got to the topic of drugs. I recalled at the first trial, Weidner accusing Larry of being "heavily under the influence of valium" during the grand jury testimony. This time he went a step further. He wondered if Larry was "addicted to valium."

With this statement Blasco became enraged. Judge Carpeneti became so angry he issued a judicial order demanding Weidner appear at a hearing and explain why he shouldn't be held in contempt of court for making the statement. Judge Carpeneti had termed the proceedings a "debacle." The judge informed Weidner that Larry Demmert "is not a government informer, was not involved in heroin use specifically or narcotics generally, and was not even charged with violating narcotics laws." Judge Carpeneti stated Weidner's argument had relied heavily on cases dealing with government informers who were addicted to heroin and, for that reason were "particularly susceptible to government pressure."

Larry had already been on the stand two weeks, remembering that his direct testimony had taken just a little more than a half an hour. Weidner was asking the same question over and over, almost like it was a recording. Judge Carpeneti had had enough. Phillip Weidner was given three additional hours to examine Larry. Judge Carpeneti told

Weidner that Larry's cross examination was to be completed by noon, March 30th, 1988 or else. Weidner again asked for a mistrial.

The next morning, Judge Carpeneti once again denied the request.

Thursday, April 7th, 1988

The jury in Peel II had been out of the courtroom as much as it had been in. It felt like the trial had been chopped into little pieces. With all the distractions, the objections and the length of time the trial had taken, it was easy to see that the jury was having a difficult time following the proceedings. If there was any advantage to this it had to be for the defense.

If anything was certain in these proceedings, it was that John Peel was still a mystery. He had not testified at the first trial and wasn't expected to testify in this trial. He had remained stoic and appeared uninterested; his only activity seemed to be scribbling notes on a legal pad. The impression was that Phillip Weidner had total control over his client. Weidner wouldn't even let Peel answer "yes" or "no" questions. During the first trial Judge Schulz remarked that John Peel "was not real quick". He said he had come to that decision based on several observations. Schulz thought peel had difficulty understanding what was going on in the courtroom.

During the second trial the prosecution thought they had found a way to make John Peel less mysterious. They had a witness that testified she had seen and spoken to the person operating the Investor skiff as it returned from the Investor fire. The prosecution had entered a motion seeking to make Peel "move, talk and try on clothing at trial." What that meant was they wanted him to walk like the skiff operator, repeat phrases said by the skiff operator and wear a flannel shirt and baseball cap like the skiff operator.

Judge Carpeneti took several cases into account before making his decision on the prosecutor's motion. Citing several cases and listening to Phillip Weidners contrary motion, he decided that John Peel would not have to walk, talk and wear the skiff operator's clothing at the trial.

Monday, April 11th

Ruth Moon the mother of Dean Moon was the last witness for the prosecution. In a very emotional testimony, she told of hearing that people had died aboard the Investor, and hoping her son was still alive. She fought back tears as she told of taking her son's dental records to the home of the Coulthursts so troopers would have a way to identify the bodies. She also chastised the investigation, when no one would tell her what happened to her son.

With Ruth Moons testimony completed, Mary Anne Henry moved to rest the prosecution's case. It was 10:15 a.m. Phillip Weidner immediately asked for a break. It was 11:00 when the court came back into session. Judge Carpeneti asked Weidner," Does the defense have evidence to present?"

"Based upon the state of the evidence and the burden of proof," Weidner responded. "The defendant rests his case."

The jury was shocked; Mary Anne Henry and Bob Blasco were stunned. The only people in the courtroom that were not surprised were John Peel and his family. Weidner had told his client and his family of his intentions before the last witness for the prosecution was finished. After his surprise decision, Weidner made a routine motion in criminal cases. He asked Judge Carpeneti for a judgment of acquittal. He stated that the state hadn't presented evidence proving John Peel committed the crime for which he was charged.

At the acquittal hearing the next day Judge Carpeneti said he was going to put off his decision until after the jury had reached its decision. Before final arguments would begin motions began flying. Weidner of course wanted a mistrial. The prosecutors wanted numerous protective orders on Phillip Weidner's closing statements; they totaled 69 orders in all. Mary Anne Henry got most of what she asked for and Weidner didn't get his mistrial. The real fireworks would happen in front of the jury, not in front of the judge. Strangely enough it would take place in front of two Judges. It seems that Judge Schulz was in Juneau on business and happened to stop by for closing arguments. He hadn't been in the courtroom long before the two sides argued and were called to a sidebar. Judge Schulz thought to himself, nothing much has changed. He also noticed how the two sides were arranged for this trial. On the prosecution side was a battery of lawyers; Henry, Blasco, Guaneli and Gullufsen. One the defense side Phillip Weidner sat alone. The message seemed clear; Phillip Weidner was single handedly taking on the State of Alaska. A real David vs.: Goliath.

Mary Anne Henry began her closing statements with what had become her standard diatribe. She used the same line and the same words she used in 1984, during her opening statements at John Peel's first trial. She had repeated them at the end of the first trial and the beginning of this trial.

"One shot fired by a gun held by the defendant John Peel started the Investor tragedy," she repeated. "After that shot, he kept shooting."

This time however she added another question "How could one person kill all those people?" She then answered her own question.

"As John Peel said it, Henry noted, "It all happened so fast." As was to be expected Phillip Weidner jumped up and interrupted Henry's closing statement by asking for a mistrial. Weidner was in his usual form. Judge Carpeneti declined to act on Weidner's request. Mary Anne Henry relinquished the rest of the closing statements to Dean Guaneli and Pat Gullufsen.

Guaneli defended one particular witness against Weidner's charges. Rebuti that the witness provided the prosecution with a convenient story about John Peel in exchange for immunity in a criminal charge that the witness had pending. "No person has immunity in advance for lying up there on the stand," Guaneli stated, adding that the witness told his father of Peel's conversation long before he faced criminal charges.

Pat Gullufsen, had drawn the job of defending Larry Demmert as well as the rest of the Libby 8 crewmembers. Gullufsen in his standard calm demeanor told a story that made sense. "It's difficult to tell the truth when you know the truth will harm someone you know," he said. Gullufsen had praise for Larry, whom he said was "brave enough" to tell all he knew.

Just like the first trial Phillip Weidner held off his closing statements until the following day.

As Weidner began his closing statement he did so by asking a question. "Will you try this case on the law and the evidence?" he asked. "Or will you try this case on conjuncture?" "We're all on trial here today," he told them. And then he said "the whole system is on trial."

Weidner patiently took the jury through every allegation he had made during the trial. He also explained why he didn't put on a defense case. He told the jury that he had expected a "more solid" case against his client.

Weidner closed his argument by telling the jury he "anticipated" their verdict. "I'm looking forward to standing here next to John Kenneth Peel." He told them. "And hearing one of you, speaking for all of you, saying not guilty nine times.

The jurors would make the final decision.

Wednesday, April 20th

The jurors were sequestered in a local hotel. They would meet for nine hours a day until they come back with a verdict. The jury room walls were lined with butcher paper, each section outlining major points of the case. Each witness had their own section on the wall. They were trying to make sense of this horrendous crime. During the trial several jurors had taken impeccable notes, all this added more information for "the wall" as it was later referred too. By day two the walls were completely covered, they had spent most of the day reviewing witness testimony.

In the early evening of day two the jury foreman decided to take the first secret ballot. The ballots were counted and the results were read. They had not reached a unanimous decision. Day three found them calling for additional evidence. They requested a tape of John Peel talking to the police in Bellingham. The tape was reviewed and still no decision. They adjourned for the day.

Day four found the jury once again pouring of witness testimony. They discussed both the defense and the prosecutions side of the case. Analyzing every important point made by both sides. Another vote was taken. It was 3:34 in the afternoon of day four. This time, they had reached a unanimous decision. This message was passed on to the bailiff and all parties were directed to return to the court room. Everyone seemed surprised that a verdict had been reached so soon.

Judge Carpeneti announced the jury's decision at 4:40 p.m. The tension in the room was almost too much to bear, a young mans life hung in the balance. After three and a half long years, and two long drawn out trials, no one wanted to wait one minute longer. Judge Carpeneti wouldn't keep them waiting.

As to the first count of murder, Judge Carpeneti announced, the jury had found John Kenneth Peel "not guilty" John Peel looked stunned, behind him applause could be heard from his family and friends. The room again became quiet as Judge Carpeneti read the next eight "not guilty" verdicts. There it was the jury had spoken. John Peel was a free man.

The saga of John Peel was far from over. Phillip Weidner in his usual arrogance asked Judge Carpeneti for a verdict of "Judgment of Innocence." One more time Judge Carpeneti refused Weidner's request. The judgment would say. Judgment of Acquittal.

Mary Anne Henry was disappointed saying "The state knows who the killer is." She also said the state would not pursue a new investigation of the Investor murders.

Many of the jurors commented after the trial. "If there was a case against John Peel to start with, the Alaska State Troopers and prosecutors blew it," said one witness. Another juror had an alternate theory for what had "really" happened. He repeated a popular idea, although the police and the prosecution had never found a shred of supporting evidence. The juror then said "the most likely cause of the Investor murders was a Mafia hit. The Investor he said "was supposedly a cocaine boat, If you wanted cocaine, you went to the Coulthurst boat."

One witness was overheard saying that "John Peel was the one person who was least likely to defend himself. And politically, they needed a fall guy, so they choose John Peel."

Many of the jurors noted that Phillip Weidner had egged on the prosecution and they had fallen for it. Mary Anne Henry especially seemed to take the bait.

It seemed like the state had sent the second string in to make the case against John Peel. Phillip Weidner against Mary Anne Henry. Two Harvard Grads squaring off against each other. The very thing movies are made of.

My Investigation

I took an early flight out of Portland, Oregon, with one stop in Seattle. I had a two hour lay over so I decided to call my old friend. He came to the airport and we had some lunch. He asked me what I was doing investigating the murders. I told him that I felt down deep that John Peel was involved; I just didn't think he could have done it alone. My friend said that it might get dangerous and I needed to be cautious. I assured him that if I felt it was getting dangerous I would back off. He grinned and knew that was a lie. He had known me too long and too well. If I found out something wasn't right, my friend knew I wouldn't let it go.

With that we said our goodbyes and I boarded my plane to Anchorage. I figured I would start by going thru the newspaper archives at the University of Alaska.

I arrived in Anchorage about 4:30 in the afternoon, and took a taxi to the Captain Cook Hotel. My room was on the eighth floor with a view of Cooke Inlet. I decided to stay in and get an early start in the morning. I ordered room service and settled in for the evening. As I relaxed and finished my dinner, I couldn't help but look out the window at the magnificent view. The mountains that surround Anchorage were still covered with snow, making the tops look like ice cream cones, the sun sets late this time of year and daylight lingers. The water of Cook Inlet was calm and the city just seemed to gravitate toward the sea. I felt an unusual calm come over me, it was a feeling I had felt before, calm just before a crisis.

The morning found me tired from the flight. I ordered some coffee to my room and showered and shaved. I looked at myself in the mirror, I was getting old, the circles under my eyes were dark, my hair was grey and my beard matched. Time had taken its toll.

This case had become an obsession; I just needed to convince myself that everything had been done to solve the murders. I just couldn't get the pictures of the children out of my mind. They deserved justice. They deserved the at least one advocate. I went to the lobby and had the bellman call me a cab. I arrived at the University library about 9:30. Finding my way to the microfiche machine, I started what would become a long and tedious task of looking thru every newspaper article that had been written about the murders. I had to get change several times it took quarters for every print I made.

By the time I was done for the day I had gone through ten dollars in quarters and a ream of paper. I was no where near the end. It looked like I would be here at least another day. I headed back to the hotel about 2:30. As I exited the cab a thought occurred to me. John Peel's attorney Phillip Weidner's office was in Anchorage; I looked the up the address of his office in the phone book at the front desk. The Anchorage phone book had several listings for attorneys; Weidner of course was listed last because of the alphabetical order. I found Phillip P. Weidner, 330 L Street. I asked the bellman how far this address might be, he told me that it was just a few blocks. I walked out the front door and turned left. As I walked my thoughts were of John Peel, the young man whose eyes caught mine in Ketchikan, the young man whose life was in the hands of the jury. A young man who seemed so cocky and self assured, so self absorbed and so defiant. Having found out through my research he had been acquitted. The first trial ending in a mistrial and the second trial ending in an acquittal. As I walked I couldn't believe that this miscarriage of justice had happened.

I found Phillip Weidners office without much problem, as I approached the front doors I felt somewhat frightened, a feeling that I was about to enter another dark chapter of this story. I approached the front desk that was hidden behind a sliding glass window, much like you see in a doctor's office. I asked the receptionist if Mr. Weidner was in and she asked me if I had an appointment, I'm sure this was her standard question. She then asked me what this might be about.

I told her I was here doing research regarding the Investor murders, with that she closed the sliding partition and walked behind a bank of files. It seemed like she was gone forever. She returned accompanied by a large mountain of a man, I knew this wasn't Weidner; I had been eye to eye with Weidner several times in Ketchikan. This looked very much like the man who had followed Larry and me during my stay in Ketchikan.

He introduced himself as Mr. Weidners private investigator. While doing so he used my first name. I hadn't given the receptionist my first name, only my last. My feeling about being frightened had now been validated. They knew about me, they knew much more than I felt comfortable with. He introduced himself by his first name only, he said his name was Phil; he invited me back to his office. I didn't know what to expect, but I followed him anyway. Sitting in a chair that was just a little shorter than his was an old trick. It was done to make one feel smaller, this strategy was done for power.

He asked about my interest in the Investor murders. He knew why I was there, he wasn't very subtle. I was going to have to summon all of my experience as a therapist and answer his questions knowing he already had the answers. Attorneys never ask questions unless they already know the answers.

I proceeded to explain that I was just doing some research regarding the outcome of the trial. I lied and told him that I was impressed with Mr. Weidner and his bulldog like tenacity. I also stated that I thought that the state didn't have much of a case against Mr. Peel, another half truth. I just wanted to know if there was any additional information that Mr. Weidner could shed on the case.

He rose from his chair and asked me to follow him. I slowly got up from my chair and made sure I was behind him as we walked out of his office. My experience told me not to allow him to get behind me. We walked down a long hallway and came to a small room at the end. Opening the door I could see it was a cramped file room, to the right I could see three tall three drawer filing cabinets, to the left several boxes maybe ten to twelve, stacked one upon another.

It was explained to me that this room was filled with nothing but documents from the Investor trial. It was overwhelming; the amount of documents was staggering. The investigator said that it would be impossible for me to go through all of this material; I knew he meant that it was off limits.

He walked me to the door and thanked me for my interest, with that he opened the door and bid me farewell. I walked back to my hotel thinking to myself that this was not going to be easy. I would have to get my information elsewhere. I felt as if I had opened something that was to remain buried forever. I was about to find out.

Arriving back in my hotel room around about 4 p.m. I was emotionally tired and my mind was racing. Again I questioned why I was doing this, maybe it was my ego, maybe I just wanted to get out of the house and not think about my wife's illness, I didn't know. I was here in Anchorage so I was going to complete this, whether I took it any further would be decided later.

I decided to take a shower, and just let the water run over me and relax. By the time I had finished showering the bathroom was full of steam, the mirrors were all fogged up. I remember thinking that they resembled my mind.

After drying myself I wrapped the towel around my waist and stepped out the bathroom door, as I did I noticed that a corner of a manila envelope was partially visible under the door. I slowly opened the door and leaned out just enough to look down the hallway in both directions. Still wrapped in a towel I didn't think it was a good Idea to stroll the hallway looking for whoever may have left it.

I picked the envelope up and closed and locked the door. I just stood there holding the envelope. I knew that whatever was inside was going to change the direction of this whole investigation. It seemed like I stood there for several moments, almost afraid to find out what the envelope contained, almost not wanting to know. Who had left this, and why? I set the envelope on the table while I dressed. Returning to the table I sat down and removed the contents of the envelope. I was right; I was stunned to find an eight page document. It was a report from the lead investigator in the Investor case. Attached to the back of the document were copies of several hand written notes, these too were from the investigator. This information would steer my efforts in an entirely different direction.

MEMORANDUM **State of Alaska**

TO: Lieutenant Robert E. Jent
Commander
Criminal Investigation Bureau

DATE: February 22, 1984

FILE NO:

TELEPHONE NO: 269-5635

FROM: Sergeant James A. Stogsdill
Major Crime Unit
Criminal Investigation Bureau

SUBJECT: Investor Investigation

[Handwritten margin notes: "This needs to go into a massey file" / "AST - Not Discoverable" / "would be better if the margin file were Xed in color"]

This memorandum will explain the recent developments regarding the Investor Homicides. It will then outline the steps I feel necessary to continue the investigation.

As you are aware, the investigation has begun to focus itself on one, John Peel, as a possible suspect in this case. Peel generally became attractive in the late summer of 1983, when numerous persons were interviewed in Craig/Ketchikan area during the anniversary of the crime. All of the investigators, who have come and gone on this case, have felt that the person(s) responsible for the killings were close, on a personal basis, to a portion of the Investor crew. As far as can be determined, the crew of the Investor were familiar with persons aboard two other vessels; the "Libby 8" and the "Cindy Sue". The crews of both of these vessels were from the Blaine/Bellingham area, as was the Investor crew. We could find no one else who knew the Investor Crew and who was in Craig at the time of the killings.

John Peel was a crewman aboard the "Libby 8". The skipper of this boat was one Larry Demmert. The "Cindy Sue" was skippered by the father of Larry Demmert, and the crews intermingled frequently.

We find that both of these boats were parked directly behind the Investor after it pulled into Craig on September 5, 1982. We know that two Investor crewmen, Moon and Keown, left the Investor right after it docked, sometime late afternoon. They went aboard the "Libby 8", where two friends, John Peel and Dawn Holmstrom, were located. These persons, along with others from the "Cindy Sue", went down into the crew quarters of the "Libby 8" and smoked marijuana and drank beer for a period of time. They then went topside and ate a meal of tacos, which had been prepared aboard the "Cindy Sue".

From this point on, we lose track of John Peel. He says he went to sleep aboard the "Libby 8" at about 6 to 8 p.m. This may or may not be true. It is disputed by Dawn Holmstrom, who says she was cleaning the boat until 8 p.m. and when she left, no one else was on board. Additionally, Larry Demmert, the skipper, says that he returned to the boat at about 10:30 p.m. to retire for the night, and he felt no one else was aboard.

We also know, through phone records and witness statements, that both Moon and Keown were at the Cold Storage laundromat at 8:30 p.m. to 9:00 p.m., making phone calls and smoking marijuana. This is important because this act is witnessed by Joe Weiss, who will be mentioned again later.

EXHIBIT PAGE 1

Investor Investigation, continued.
February 22, 1984
Page Two.

Additionally, we know that the other Investor crewmen, Stewart and Heyman, are also at the laundromat making phone calls following those of Moon and Keown. There is no evidence of intoxication or marijuana use from the witness who sees this act.

After all four of the Investor crewmen leave the Cold Storage laundromat, (at their separate times) the only indication as to their whereabouts comes from Larry Demmert, who says that when he returns to the "Libby 8" for the evening (10:30 p.m.), he sees several persons aboard the Investor "partying". Recall that Demmert felt that no one else is aboard the "Libby 8".

At about this same time, Dawn Holmstrom is at the Hill Bar. She had indicated to Moon and Keown earlier that she would see them there. They were not there. Holmstrom doesn't recall seeing John Peel there either. She sat with some crewmembers from the F/V "Glacier Bay". This was confirmed by those crewmembers.

All of the above I feel leads to one conclusion. If the Investor crew are in town and are drinking and smoking, they would be in the company of John Peel or Dawn Holmstrom. Holmstrom admits some sexual involvement with Moon, so they are closer than just "friends". Also, John Peel worked with Moon on board the "Kit", the boat previously owned by Mark Coulthurst before the Investor, for two years. One could conclude that they were more than acquaintances. In fact, Peel indicated in a statement taken a year after his first contact that he had furnished marijuana to Moon and Keown - an indication that they would be expected to be together.

John Peel, of course, worked for Mark Coulthurst on the F/V "Kit". Peel was "fired" in the late fall of 1981 by Mark Coulthurst. This firing is described by those who were there as generally amiable. Peel had apparently become lazy and late for work and Coulthurst grew tired of it. Peel describes the incident as "quitting" when it was obvious that Coulthurst was "going for the gusto" and would no longer give bonuses. Coulthurst also wanted Peel to quit smoking dope on the boat and Peel says it was a sign of things to come, so they parted company.

Basically, Peel has no alibi for Sunday evening, September 5, the time when the persons aboard the Investor are killed. One of the difficulties faced in this case was the argument concerning the reason for the boat being burned two days after the killing and in broad daylight. This act makes considerable sense, if you are a surviving crewman and would be conspicuous by your absence. If a non-crewman is responsible the reason for burning the boat becomes less obvious.

It is a reasonable certainty that the Investor was supposed to sink after being moved from North Cove to Fish Egg Island. All of the valves in the engine room were in the open position, an unusual formation. This failing, burning the boat became an alternative. Additionally, accelerant was brought aboard. Available fuel was not used.

Investor Investigation, continued
February 22, 1984
Page Three.

Contact with the person operating the Investor skiff and coming from the burning boat, by four persons, is where the four original composites came from. They generally agree in their descriptions of the person although the drawings vary in appearance.

In the latter part of 1983, a letter was received from Joe Weiss of Eureka, California. Weiss was personally contacted and shown a photo lineup containing a picture of John Peel. Weiss picked out Peel's photo as being "most like" the person he saw. Weiss saw and spoke to a person getting out of the Investor skiff on Monday morning, after the boat was moved from North Cove to Fish Egg Island. Very likely the murderer. His clothing description matches that of the four people who see the person in the skiff on Tuesday afternoon, after the fire begins on the Investor. Weiss sees the person <u>without</u> glasses. The wearing of the glasses on Tuesday appears to be an attempt at disguise, as they weren't needed on Monday. The glasses are similar to those owned by Mark Coulthurst. It should be noted that Weiss waffles between Peel and Heyman during the latter part of the interview. Peel and Heyman are similar in appearance. The profile photo of Heyman was a good quality photo while those of Peel were poor quality.

Most important; however, is the fact that Weiss saw both Moon and the killer. He was able to definitely say that the person who got off the skiff on Monday morning was not Moon or Keown. This is the first positive information that a crewman from the Investor was not involved in the killings - or if a crewman is involved, he has an accomplice.

Naturally, the conclusion to draw is that whether or not a crewman is involved - Peel must be knowledgeable of the events; either as a principal or accomplice.

As previously discussed, we cannot account for the whereabouts of John Peel on Sunday evening the 5th of September, during which time the killings occur. Can we account for his whereabouts when the Investor begins to burn? No. Peel says he was going to the post office with Dawn Holmstrom when they see the smoke from the fire. Dawn Holmstrom generally agrees with Peel. Larry Demmert indicates that he and his crew, including Peel, were working on the net on the dock. A couple of hours before the fire, Demmert indicates that Peel disappeared. Demmert assumed that Peel had gone up to the Craig Inn for a drink, because that's where he is found later on that evening. So, on Tuesday just prior to the fire, we are not sure where Peel is located.

One would think that this is a question easily answered by showing John Peel photographs to the witnesses, who encounter the operator of the Investor's skiff coming from the burning boat. This was done and the results are similar. Keeping in mind that these witnesses are trying to I.D. a person they saw for a few moments over a year and some months ago. <u>Jan Kittleston</u> -- "This picture (Peel's) looks more

EXHIBIT B PAGE 3

Investor Investigation, continued.
February 22, 1984
Page Four.

like my composite than any other picture I've seen." Sue Domenowske --
"He looks similar but the hair on the person I saw was darker."
Paul Page -- "He looks similar, but the person I saw looked younger."
Bruce Anderson has not been contacted. Ironically, the composite
that Anderson had drawn and that was never published or shown to the
public, looks identical to the actual John Peel photographs taken
during an interview in November, 1983, down to the way the clothing
was worn.

Interestingly enough, it was learned that the "Libby 8" had aboard
two rifles which matched the caliber of the murder weapon, .22 long
rifle. One of these belonged to Larry Demmert. The other belonged
to a "Libby 8" crewman by the name of McQuistan. These guns were
surrendered by their owners to Bellingham Police and subsequentty
sent to the F.B.I. for comparison with the bullet fragments from the
bodies. The results were a definite no on the McQuistan gun and an
inconclusive on the Demmert gun, leaving the possibility of it still
being the murder weapon.

The next logical step would then be to fit John Peel with the facts
of the crime, as they are known, to see how he compares with a crewmember. We must keep in mind the fact that a crewmember of the Investor
may be involved because remains of two unidentified crewmen may not be
present.

Probably the best way to do this is to list the reasons why Peel could
be responsible, and then list reasons which indicate he may not be
responsible for the crime.

A. Facts which indicate John Peel involved in the killings aboard
the Investor:

1. He is in Craig at the time of the killings.
2. He is one of the last persons to see Moon and Keown alive.
3. At the time of the killings (Sunday night) his whereabouts
are unknown.
4. He personally knows everyone on the Investor, except Heyman.
5. His vessel was moored directly behind the Investor during
the killings.
6. He had access to like murder weapon.
7. He is familiar with fishing boat and skiff operation, but not
the peculiarities of the Investor - hence, the attempt to
sink the boat, the broken skiff ramp, etc.
8. He matches the description as to size, weight, hair length,
eyes, speech.
9. He is identified by Joe Weiss as "most like" the person
seen operating the skiff.
10. He is described as "similar" by the other witnesses - to the
person they saw coming from the burning boat.
11. He disappears from his work place for two hours prior to
the Investor fire.
12. He is the only person of the "Libby 8", "Cindy Sue" crews
who shows no interest in going out to see the Investor burn.

EXHIBIT 6 PAGE 4

Investor Investigation, continued.
February 22, 1984
Page Five.

13. He readily admits being "stoned" the night of the killings.
14. He had a readily available place to "hide" while things quieted down.
15. He escaped detection because he merely returned to "normal" and blended in.
16. He appears on flight manifest to leave Craig immediately after police contact, rather than going home on the "Cindy Sue" as planned.
17. There is open dislike on Mark Coulthurst part towards Peel in P[ ] opinion.

B. Facts indicating John Peel **not** involved in the killings aboard the Investor:

1. He indicates he was in bed by 8 p.m. because he was "stoned".
2. Dawn Holmstrom says Peel was with her, going to the Craig post office, when the Investor fire broke out.
3. No obvious motive for the deed.
4. No obvious reason for him to burn the boat since he wouldn't be conspicuous by his absence aboard.
5. He was not with Moon and Keown at the Cold Storage laundromat at 8:30 p.m. to 9:00 p.m. Sunday night - indiciating that they had parted company.
6. Was not identified by any of the witnesses who were taken to the Hill Bar to view him.
7. Dean Moon was "seen" in San Francisco by a witness who had worked with him in early 1982.

That generally outlines the case up to this point, especially regarding John Peel. There are no other suspects in this case, however remote. If it turns out that Peel just looks good, but is not knowledgeable or involved, then the truth of the matter is I start from the beginning again in hopes of a miracle.

The second part of this memorandum will outline what I feel needs to be done next and by whom. There is, simply, no physical evidence in this case. There are no eye witnesses, with the possible exception of Joe Weiss, who will commit themselves to an identification after this period of time. The F.B.I. has said that the bullet fragments from the bodies will never be positively matched to a specific weapon. I suspect there will always be two of the crewmen who cannot be positively identified. The boat was burned so badly and was awash with high tide so often that physical evidence was limited. The fact that it was arson is unquestioned. With the exception of a plastic nozzle from a gas can with no prints - there was no evidence in the Investor's skiff.

Suffice it to say that a confession with collaborating facts is imperative to conclude this case. Without it, there is no case. Therefore everything should be directed to that end. Since the time of the offense, there has been only one indication that a crewmember might still be alive and that was the sighting of Moon in San Francisco. However, despite considerable effort, no one else could be found who

EXHIBIT 6 PAGE 5

Investor Investigation, continued.
February 22, 1984
Page Six.

saw Moon in that area. The reported sighting was brief and without contact. I am continuing under the assumption that a crewmember was not the person seen in the Investor's power skiff.

These are the steps I feel necessary to find out one way or the other what John Peel knows or what he did regarding this crime.

1. At a specified date, begin media coverage of the Investor investigation. We have a good quality television type video tape, which can be distributed to stations in Southeast Alaska and the Bellingham/Blaine area. In addition, do radio and newspaper interviews regarding the investigation. This has two purposes; a) solicit any information from persons who haven't come forward as yet, b) cause John Peel to begin thinking about the events and cause other people to talk to Peel about it. Hopefully, this will help prepare him for upcoming interrogation.

2. While the media is spreading the story around, it will be necessary to bring Joe Weiss from California to Bellingham. Once there, put Weiss into a position where he will be able to see John Peel and hopefully identify him. Even though Weiss has seen a photo of Peel, it was of such poor quality that I don't feel it will ruin any subsequent identification. Weiss is probably the best witness of the five in terms of recall and expression. He is a graduate student at Humboldt University. If <u>anyone</u> can come close to a positive I.D. on the person in the skiff, it will be Joe Weiss. This step cannot be eliminated. Whether or not Weiss identifies Peel, I feel it would be derelict not to afford him the opportunity. <u>Any</u> form of identification of Peel could be used as a lever at a later interrogation.

3. The next step involves surveillance. It will be done simultaneously with steps one and two. I want someone who Peel does not know to frequent the same places that Peel does. I feel it will be necessary to know little things about John Peel; his favorite beer, what brand of cigarette does he smoke, what slang words does he use, what does he like to talk about, how good is he at playing pool, etc. - all of these things can be very useful when it comes to interrogation time. Additionally, some surveillance will give me some insight as to Peel's activity, so that I can "accidently" bump into him at the gas station or convenience store. (He knows me from last interview).

4. While steps one, two and three are underway, several of the people who were closest to Peel should be brought in for interrogation and polygraph. This of course means a polygraph operator from here going to Bellingham. In addition, I would like to keep the possibility open for putting Peel on the polygraph at some point in his questioning. Other persons who would be polygraphed include Dawn Holmstrom, whose story changes with each telling. Brian Polinkus, crewman on "Libby 8" and close

EXHIBIT B PAGE 6

Investor Investigation, continued.
February 22, 1984
Page Seven.

    friend of Peel. This may be the one person Peel would tell of the killings, if he told anyone at all.

5. When we feel ready, bring in John Peel for questioning. This is a now or never situation. I feel we will only get one chance at John Peel. Once we point the finger at him, if we walk away without a confession or admissions or all the information he has, there will <u>not</u> be a second chance if something comes up later, this is <u>my</u> opinion. This step will take careful planning and execution, if a confession is hoped for. I can't put enough emphasis on the importance of this interrogation. Additionally, I don't feel I have the refined ability to properly interrogate John Peel. This ability exists in the Department and should be used in this case. Even a team of interrogators who have worked together successfully (example: McCann/Stockard) should be carefully considered. I have contacted the local F.B.I., who will arrange for an interview analysis from the Behavioral Sciences Unit in Quantico. Hopefully, that information could assist the interrogator.

Generally, that is my plan of attack. It is of course flexible depending on what the person conducting the interrogation feels might enhance his chances.

I have spoken with Mary Ann Henry, the District Attorney on this case, and she will be present in Bellingham during this sequence of events. She will observe and advise where needed. When we do have a confession, she will make the necessary warrant requirements and prepare for extradition.

What I have outlined above is what I consider our <u>best</u> <u>shot</u> at John Peel. I would expect the entire procedure to consume at least 10 days of time, all in Bellingham, Washington. At a minimum, the following persons are required for successful completion:

1.   Myself
2.   McCann/Stockard (interrogators)

I would feel very comfortable with that number of people. I would recommend Sergeant Stockard as the polygraph examiner.

There is a polygraph examiner at the Bellingham Police Department. He has just graduated from Polygraph School. He has also aided with the Investor case (Detective Dave McNeill). His use would depend on how busy the detective unit is at the time. Additionally, without our own surveillance person, we would probably run into complications trying to borrow people for this purpose.

I expect that we are ready to do this whenever all parties, who are going to travel to Bellingham, can get together to discuss the case

Investor Investigation, continued.
February 22, 1984
Page Eight.

at length and plan in detail.

I realize that the purse strings will have to be stretched to their breaking point. However, this needs to be done and it deserves nothing less than our best effort.

I am available if you or anyone wishes to discuss any aspect of this case.

cc: Mary Ann Henry, Esq., D.A., Ketchikan
    Case File

JAS/sab

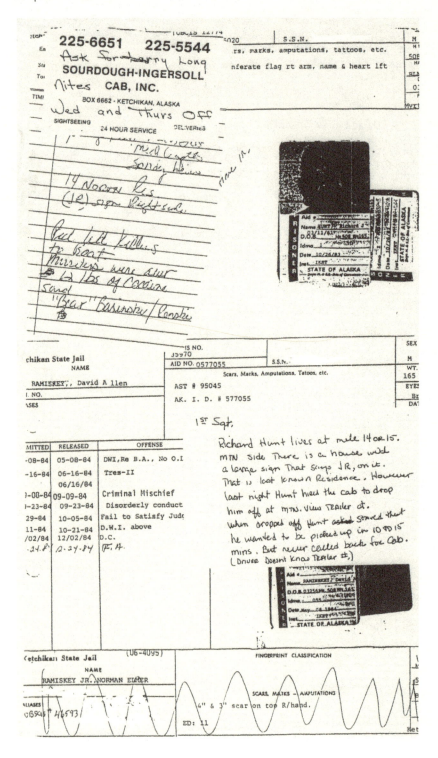

I now realized that I had opened Pandora's Box. Not only did I know the key witness, but I also knew who had murdered the family and the crew.

I sat there stunned, the more I read, the more I started to put the pieces together. I knew the envelope had been delivered by Phillip Weidners investigator. I had to talk to him again. My mind reeling, my stomach churning. I now had information that was withheld at trial, information that could re-open this case. I was holding documents that with what I personally knew, would now cast a shadow on the whole case. Two trials, millions of dollars later, apparent cover-ups, buried information and lies; it was all here in front of me.

I called Phillip Weidners office, I asked to speak to the investigator, and I told the receptionist my name. I was put on hold. A voice came on the line and I recognized it as the investigators, all I said was "we need to meet" he told me where and when. It seemed that we both had the same idea, meet somewhere public, somewhere crowded. We met in the lobby of the hotel. I had several questions, some he was hesitant to answer; with others he was very open. He said that I should look at the second trial transcripts; he also said I should look at the personal relationships of all the legal teams. He wouldn't tell me anything that might insinuate wrong doing, but he was adamant.

I ask him why the message "Get out now" he said there was a lot of powerful people that had become aware of my visit and they were somewhat upset. I ask him why he was doing this for me, why the information, his response surprised me. The truth needs to come out, I too think of those children everyday. I asked him the most important question of all, "did John Peel do this?" he wouldn't answer, he just nodded in an affirming manner, I then told him my gut says that Peel wasn't alone; he smiled and said "follow your gut". With that he rose from his chair and once again said "leave as soon as you can".

That's the last time I was to see him. I returned to my room and called my wife. I told her of my new discovery; there was a long pause on her end. "What are you going to do?" she asked. I told her I wasn't done with my library research and I wanted to get all the information I could before I came home. She knew that I wasn't going to be chased out of town; she wished me luck and told me to be careful. The next morning found me in the University Library on the microfiche machine once again. I found many more articles relating to the murders, I copied all I could and returned to the hotel to pack. Entering my room I noticed that things had been moved around on my desk, my suitcase had been moved and items in the bathroom were rearranged. Someone had been in there looking for something, looking for the manila envelope and its contents was my first thought.

Having been around this block before, I had taken the envelope and the memos with me to the library. I made copies and mailed the original home from the University mailroom.

I packed and caught the first plane bound for Seattle. It left in an hour. I caught a cab and just made the flight. Once aboard the plane I could exhale. I watched Anchorage disappear below me, my mind was exploding, my heart was racing and I knew I was in the middle of something much bigger than I was. I also knew that it needed to be done; I just wondered why it was me that was destined to do it.

The flight would take two and a half hours to Seattle, an hour lay over, and then on to Portland; from there it would be another hour and a half drive to my home, arriving there late in the evening. It would have been a long day by any stretch of the imagination, however this day seemed like it would never end. Pulling into my driveway I noticed the time was 11:30 p.m. I was exhausted both physically and mentally.

The next day found me up early and sorting out all the information I had obtained in Anchorage. I cleared off an entire wall in my office, taking down pictures and plaques, it was almost like I was removing my past and making way for a future, an uncertain future at best. After almost two hours, I had papered the entire wall with newspaper clippings from dozens of papers, articles from magazines; People Magazine had a great article in their September 12th 1983 issue. It contains one of the only pictures of the actual fire aboard the Investor.

I stepped back and looked at the entire wall; I had tried to place each clipping in the order in which it had been written. Many of them repeated the same information, however I needed to see through each reporter's eyes, I needed to feel the moment, and I had to get a hold of the emotion at the time. Many of the articles were written about the first trial, I read these with some interest, but having been there I was able to discern some bias in the reporting. I was most interested in the second trial, not having been there I had only Larry's account to rely on and I knew how disappointed he was with the outcome. I knew I would have to obtain the trial transcripts of the second trial.

I really didn't want to go back to Alaska right away, but I had to get the transcripts from the second trial. They were available at the State Library in Juneau. I called the library and they said that they were indeed available and I could have them gathered for my inspection, they said there were quite a few boxes of testimony. I told them I would get back to them in the next few days as to when I would be there.

I told my wife of my dilemma, and as usual she had a suggestion. She recommended that I contact the library again and ask them if they knew any students at the University that might be willing to help with project. A good idea, so I called the librarian back and indeed she said that many students place ads on their board looking for work, she gave me some names and phone numbers and I again said I would be contacting her as to when I would want the boxes made available.

I called the first number I had been given, it was that of a grad-student named Marcie, I explained what I wanted done and the time frame that I needed the work completed. She said that she had a few days off from school and would be willing to do the job. I told her that I wanted every single page of the trial transcript copied and sent to me in Oregon. I said I would send her the money for the coping as well as pay her one hundred dollars per day. She seemed more than satisfied with this arrangement. I felt that she could get this done in about three days. I wired her the money and told her to let me know daily as to the progress.

It took longer than I expected, Marcie said that there were over six boxes of transcripts and progress was slow. On the fifth day she called and said she had completed the job and was preparing to ship the boxes via Air. She said they would arrive in five business days. I thanked Marcie and said I would send her a little extra for her time and effort. As promised six boxes arrived in five days, Marcie had labeled each box individually from day one of the second trial. It took almost three days and nights to read the second trial transcripts.

Again the information that I had uncovered was withheld and never mentioned in the second trial. Why was the drug angle not followed up more vigorously? Bear Pierskie was never mentioned even though the Troopers had information from him. Why wasn't the eight page memo that I had been given allowed into evidence? These were questions I would have to get answers for. It was obvious that my investigation had already uncovered some very disturbing facts. People in powerful places with skeletons in the closets were not going to be happy.

I said to myself Fuck-em.

⤻

It had been sometime since I had spoken to Mark's girlfriend. I knew she had moved back to Seattle and had started her life over. I called her parents and they were very glad to hear from me. After talking for awhile and catching up on our lives, I asked them for her phone number.

The phone rang several times, at the other end was a voice of a young boy, I asked if his mother was home?, with some hesitation he said no she will be back any minute, she just stepped out. I knew that was a standard answer and I understood why. I asked him if he would take my number and have her call me when she returned, he agreed, I slowly repeated my number and he said he would have her call me.

I didn't expect a return call so soon, it was just a matter of minutes. She was so excited to here form me and couldn't stop thanking me for all my wife and I had done for she and her son. We talked about what had taken place in our lives over the past few years. Her son was now twelve years old and doing well. She had returned to work in the Seattle base and they lived just a few blocks from her parents, which made things a lot easier raising her son. I mentioned that I was doing research into the mass murders aboard a fishing vessel in Craig Alaska. I told her that I thought it was drug related, and also mentioned that Bear Pierskies name had been brought up. There was a long silence on her end of the line. I came right out and asked her if she could remember if Mark had been in Craig during the time of the murders. She paused, her answer surprised me. She said "on several occasions I had supplied Mark free passes to Craig"; she couldn't remember for sure if he had been there during the dates I had mentioned.

Her next statement again surprised me. She said that "one of Marks partners had a float plane. She said that they may have used it for trips to Craig".

One more time it had became clear that the investigators had missed an important clue. The troopers had canvassed the airport, looked at flight manifests, questioned attendants, checked the ferry terminal, and explored all avenues of escape. In Alaska, float planes are as common as automobiles, this would have provided a perfect escape for someone who needed to get out of Craig undetected. It also would never have to appear in Craig itself. A floatplane could have easily maneuvered up to the Investor as she lay at anchor off of Fish Egg Island and removed the actual murderer. This was all coming together in a very ugly scenario.

I needed to put this information in some sort of order. I need answers. I would have to create a timeline, reconstruct the murder scene and place the new information and evidence into a formula that would fit with the new information.

Creating the timeline would not be difficult. The investigators had done a relatively good job tying together the events. The witnesses would be harder. I would need to at least make an effort to re-construct the actual crime scene. I would need to find a 58 foot Delta Marine. I called my friend in Seattle. It wasn't long before he found the exact boat. I asked him if he knew a

Firearm expert that could help me with the single gunman theory. Knowing my friend and his connections, I knew he would find a reputable source. I told him I would come to Seattle in the next few days.

The Delta Marine boat was perfect, she was moored in North Seattle and the owner was more than happy to let us aboard. When I told him what I was doing his response was "I knew the Coulthursts, you take as much time as you need."

My friend had found a former ballistics and firearm expert who retired from the FBI several years ago. It seems their paths had crossed in another lifetime. I didn't ask. We made arrangements to meet early the next morning. Before going to my hotel my friend and I made plans to meet for dinner that night. The restaurant was one of my favorites in Seattle. I had run these streets when I was a kid and knew my way around Seattle. I had met my friend here in the late 60's. We both had the same intentions and found ourselves in running gun battles down the alleys of Chinatown. It was good that neither one of us were very good shots at the time. As with any adversaries we had gained a respect of the streets and of one another.

We met in Chinatown for dinner. The restaurant hadn't changed a bit. It still catered to the local Chinese. The restaurant had been here long before I was, it was known for its discretion. It would be nothing to see local dignitaries, sitting at a round table with local gangsters. The air was heavy with cigar smoke and food cooking in gigantic woks. Of course the menu had two prices, one in Chinese and one for the rest of the world. I had been coming here off and on for 25 years. As I walked in the door I was immediately greeted by an old friend. He had worked here for over thirty years; he had come directly from China in 1945 with his parents. No one seemed to know who owned the restaurant; it just seemed to be the same people, doing the same jobs forever. Every once in awhile you would see a new waiter, some of the faces had changed in the kitchen, but mostly the same people, just older, just wiser. I had known my friend for years; he had told me that the basement of this place held several stories. It was rumored to be a gambling hall, a whorehouse, a bootlegging place way back when. It was also rumored to have housed illegal Chinese immigrants that were smuggled into Seattle aboard freighters bound for the west coast. All of these stories I tended to believe.

We were quickly shown to a table, much to the displeasure of the patrons who had been waiting in a line outside for several minutes.

Once seated it was easy to see nothing had changed. My friend came to the table with a menu. I told him to just bring us what he would suggest. He bowed and smiled, I think he even chuckled as he walked away. I suddenly reflected on my gastric encounter in Taipei. I hoped it wasn't going to be a repeat.

My friend and I made some small talk; he quickly changed the subject to my investigation. He asked me what direction it was taking. I briefly filled him in with my new information, he wasn't surprised of my findings, he did show some interest when I mentioned the "mafia" type hit and my reason for it. I told him I was not sure how to connect all the dots. He suggested that I just point out the new evidence, the new theories and let the readers figure it out. "People would come to their own conclusions anyway." "Just lay out what you have found. Trust your readers."

The dinner was delicious, no surprises. We called it a night and went our separate ways. We agreed to meet at the boat the next morning at 9 am. My friend said he would pick up the gun expert.

⌇

The morning found us climbing aboard the identical boat that the Coulthursts had owned. She was a beautiful working boat. Everything had its place and nothing was aboard that wasn't needed to do the job. Lines were curled on the deck; nets were neatly stacked on the stern. All the hoists and winches were carefully maintained. The old saying "if the winch isn't turning, we ain't earning" came to mind.

The boat was preparing to head to Southeast Alaska in just a few days for the hearing opening. This fishery is vital to a years earnings, a season can be made or broken in just a few hours.

The captain met us on board. He showed us the working areas and then told us to take as much time as needed inside the vessel. Climbing a few step we entered the galley. I could tell right away that just the three of us in here at one time made for a crowded space. Off of the Galley to the starboard side lay the stateroom where Mrs. Coulthurst and her daughter were reported to sleep. To the left of this small space were the crew's quarters. This space was cramped, three small bunks on each side of the quarters, a small walkway between. There would have been no way that all six crewmembers would have been able stand in this space at once. Six more stairs upward led us to the helm. This space was more open. It contained a small couch actually it was more like a cushioned bench. This is where the small boy was believed to have been found, remembering only ashes had been found. It was the hub of the boat. All the controls and electronics were at the skippers fingertips. The view from the windows allowed the skipper an unobstructed sightline to the working deck as well as the bow of the vessel. This was the area that had melted under the intense heat and collapsed to the lower quarters. All the while I was thinking to myself that something just didn't fit. Going back down to the galley area I just couldn't believe that one man had created so much carnage. Arriving back in the galley, I found my friend and the ballistic expert taking exact measurements. I just stepped out of the way. I knew that they had much more experience in matters such as this. They measured the galley where John Coulthurst and his pregnant wife had been found. They then measured the stateroom where another body was found. It was believed to be the remains of the young daughter.

They then found their way to the crew's quarters. This space was cramped and narrow as I had previously stated. I wondered to myself why they were taking so much time in this area. I had found it strange that all six crewmembers were found in this area. I had questioned why six young, strong fishermen, had not been able to overtake a lone gunman. Why one or more weren't able to do something after hearing the first of many gunshots.

I was soon to find out that my friend also had questions.

We had been on board almost two hours, and were finally finished. We had taken pictures, taken measurements, paced off distances and placed ourselves in not only the deceased victim's positions but also where we thought the gunman had to stand to carry out these brutal murders. We thanked the captain and departed to my hotel to discuss our findings. On the drive back to the hotel we hardly spoke. I was feeling as if I had been in a time warp. I could almost hear the screams; smell the gunpowder and feel the heat of the fire. I could tell my friend and our consultant were deep it thought. The silence was almost deafening.

Pulling up to the hotel we had valet park the car. We then went directly to my room and ordered some coffee. Clearing off the table, my friend spread out their findings. I could see from the notes and measurements, that this was going to be more new information.

The coffee arrived and we sat down for a minute still in silence. The first to speak was the ballistics expert. He spoke first about the galley area. He said although the area was large enough to wield a 22 caliber rifle, it didn't lend itself enough room to reload and proceed to the other areas of the boat. I told him of my theory of a second gunman.

He politely asked me to wait until he finished with his summary. I apologized for the interruption. He continued. "The measurement of the crew quarters leads me to believe that the crew was helpless to react. The stateroom was accessible to gunshots without much problem if the door had been open". I remembered the young girl had always wanted it left ajar, just to feel safe and closer to her mom and dad, while they were in the galley.

My friend who had been unusually silent finally spoke. He said "let's cut the shit here. These people were murdered by more than one person. It is impossible for all six crew members to not react. At least one or more would have gotten to one lone gunman. The only way this could have happened was if there had been somebody else on board maybe more than one other person. It then would have been possible only if the crew had been held at gunpoint by a second gunman. He wouldn't have had to do the shooting, just hold them in place".

The ballistics expert spoke. "I agree with this scenario, I would add however, that one person would have had to reload at least twice. At least with the information provided by the troopers regarding the number of gunshots they believe were fired. This again confirmed my theory that more than one person was on board the boat at the time of the murders".

I then asked both of them what they had thought of the "mafia hit" theory that the defense tried to present. Both reacted at the same time. My friend responded "the murders seemed too precise and specific to have been a crime done spontaneously". The ballistics expert agreed. He went on to add, "Reports seem to say that all on board had been shot execution style. This was not a random shooting. I can't believe that this wasn't investigated with more thought to details".

I then asked them both the question I have asked myself a thousand times. I asked if either of them thought there might have been a cover up. I asked them both if they actually thought that the State Troopers could have missed what we had uncovered?

Almost in unison they answered "no". My friend said there was "no way any half trained detective could have missed this information". The ballistics expert went one step further. He said "in all his years with the FBI he had never come across such incompetence".

I knew my friend had been in similar situations, and had first hand knowledge of close range encounters. I trusted his input. How could I argue with an expert in firearms? My suspicions had been validated.

John Peel wasn't alone. The next question is who else had been on board the Investor that gruesome night?

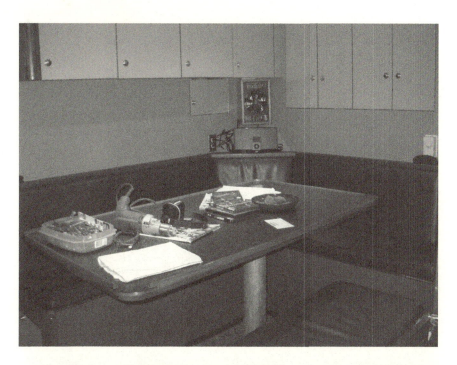

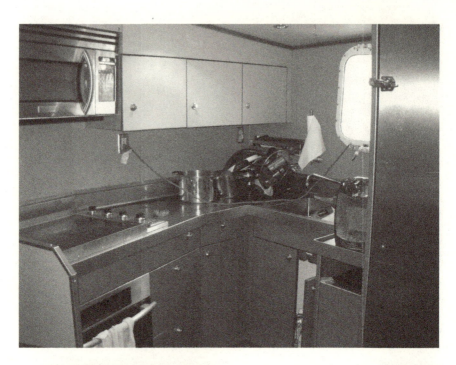

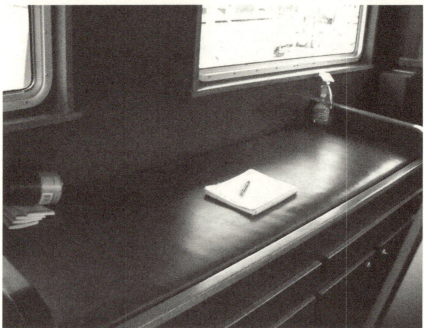

Arriving back at home I tried to put everything into perspective. I arranged the photo's I had taken a board the boat. The galley, the crew's quarters, and the wheelhouse where the young boy's ashes were reported to have been located. With these in front of me I began to see that it would have been impossible for one shooter to swing a rifle around and continue his rampage. Someone else had held the crew captive and in place. I believe that John Peel was involved. The note the investigators had found said that "John Peel led the murderers to the Investor."

A clear motive for the murders was never established, the State tried to say it was a spontaneous eruption between John Peel and Mark Coulthurst.

The note that said John Peel led the murderers to the boat, also stated that the murders were over missing cocaine. The prosecutors would never allow any of the drug theory into evidence. John Peel's attorney desperately tried to enter the drug theory only to be rebuked at every turn. The information came directly from a very powerful union leader who himself had strong drug ties. The investigators' also had information on a person from Anchorage who was involved with moving large amounts of cocaine from the lower "48." Once again the State never allowed anything that resembled a drug angle to be allowed. Why was that?

It's quite obvious that whoever did the killings made a statement. A statement that stealing drugs would not be tolerated.

Powerful people had tried to derail my investigation. The man who was identified as giving the information to the Troopers was also involved with overseeing of the trust account with the Labor Union in Alaska. His partner with the trust fund is now a State Senator in Alaska. Powerful people in powerful places can make people disappear.

I also find it very strange that most of the Troopers were reassigned to various parts of Alaska. Trooper Anderson left the troopers and opened a fishing lodge in Klawock. Sergeant Stogsdill retired to become a halibut fisherman. Judge Schulz retired and became a minister. Judge Schulz was asked if he thought the Peel trial would have turned out differently had it been tried before a judge, he said he doesn't know. He said he has given it much thought, and believes that John Peel would have been convicted had it been a civil matter. Others went on to retire with huge advancements in short periods of time. Some went from homicide to narcotics; others went from narcotics to investigators'. Others just seemed to disappear into the system. Only one Trooper remained on the Investor case. The largest unsolved mass murder in Alaska State history just faded away.

Two trials and millions of tax payer's dollars later still no answers. Trial number one ending in a mistrial. The first Judge dismissed from presiding over trial number two because of the defense attorneys affair with the judges law clerk. At the same time the District Attorney Mary Anne Henry was reported to be having an affair with one of the State Troopers who was involved with investigating the murders. Some say she was being fed information that led the evidence away from the actual killers.

As a writer I always ask "why". John Peel was left alive if it was a statement killing? Why was he left to take the fall? My answer is that the killers never thought he would be a suspect, or he would never be convicted based on the evidence. The memo from the State Trooper to the district attorney stated clearly that unless Peel confessed they would not be able to convict him, yet they tried him twice. Did the killers know this? Did they have this information?

Larry Demmert said that he was sure it was John Peel standing on the dock with what appeared to be a rifle and gas can. To this date he has not waivered. Several witnesses described a man that "looked like John Peel". In my investigation I found that the drug dealer from Anchorage also fits the description of the man seen aboard the investor as it pulled away from the dock the night of the murders.

Mark A Ward fits the description. He also is involved with the union leader, he has the ability to come and go undetected. He is known to use fishing boats to smuggle drugs up from Bellingham.

I do believe that the Coulthursts had no knowledge of any drug activity aboard the investor. I believe that one of the crew members had ripped off the missing drugs. I believe that John Peel was forced to provide information and direct the killers to the Investor. Once on board the mayhem began. The Coulthursts denying any involvement, the crew members unable to respond, and the killers just executed them at will. A tragedy for sure.

THE END

Epilogue?

Do I believe that this book will make a difference? Probably not. Do I believe that the case will be re-opened? Probably not. What I do believe is that I have come as close to solving this case as I can. I have raised many unanswered questions. I have opened many closets that contain powerful figures. I have answered some questions that for over twenty years have been silenced. There can be no real epilog until this case is solved.

    Post Script: In 2006 Andy (Bear) Piereski was found dead at his fishing Lodge. His death was quickly ruled an accident.
    Mark A Ward has disappeared, totally off the grid.

Made in the USA
Coppell, TX
23 July 2021